Vocabulary Development for ESL Students: Beginner

Lisa Solski

W0007320

BRIEF OVERVIEW: This workbook uses simple strategies to teach Beginner Level ESL students 240 everyday words and incorporate them into daily situations.

Published in Canada by:
On The Mark Press
Belleville, ON
www.onthemarkpress.com

Funded by the Government of Canada

Canada

At A Glance

Learning Expectations	Recognizes New Words	Uses a dictionary, thesaurus, and personal dictionary.	Uses flash cards and finds a helper to practise pronunciation.	Divides words into syllables.	Examines root words, prefixes, and suffixes.	Uses context when reading.
Recognizes new vocabulary words when they are presented.	●					
Uses a dictionary, thesaurus and Personal Dictionary to learn new words.		●				
Uses flash cards and finds a helper to practise pronunciation.			●			
Divides words into syllables.				●		
Examines root words, prefixes, and suffixes.					●	
Uses context when reading.						●

OTM18112   ISBN: 9781770788718 © On The Mark Press

Table of Contents

Teacher Assessment Rubric

Student's Name: _____

Put a check mark ✔ in the box that indicates the student's level of achievement.

Level 1	requires assistance, inconsistent effort, shows limited understanding of concepts
Level 2	requires minimal assistance, shows limited understanding of concepts
Level 3	independent, consistent effort, shows general understanding of concepts
Level 4	independent, consistent effort, shows thorough understanding of concepts

Criteria	Level 1	Level 2	Level 3	Level 4
Recognizes new vocabulary words when they are presented.				
Uses a dictionary, thesaurus and Personal Dictionary to learn new words.				
Uses flash cards and finds a helper to practise pronunciation.				
Divides words into syllables.				
Examines root words, prefixes, and suffixes.				
Uses context when reading.				

OTM18112 ISBN: 9781770788718 © On The Mark Press

Student Self-Assessment Rubric

Name: _____ Date: _____

Put a check mark ✔ in the box that best describes your performance.
Then add your points.

Expectations	1 Needs Improvement	2 Sometimes	3 Frequently	4 Always/ almost always	Points
Recognizes new vocabulary words when they are presented.					
Uses a dictionary, thesaurus and Personal Dictionary to learn new words.					
Uses flash cards and finds a helper to practise pronunciation.					
Divides words into syllables.					
Examines root words, prefixes, and suffixes.					
Uses context when reading.					

Acquiring New Vocabulary

Unfamiliar vocabulary prevents English language learners from understanding what they read. Chances are they often ask themselves questions like this when they read.

- What is this word?
- Have I ever seen this word before?
- What are the parts of this word?
- What does this word mean?
- How should I use this word when writing?

This book is designed to help English learners become more successful in understanding and using English words. Experts agree that **reading, writing, speaking and listening** are the keys to developing a better vocabulary. One of the many frustrations students encounter when **reading** new material is unfamiliar vocabulary. It is not uncommon while **reading** a passage for students to come across several unfamiliar words that prevent them from understanding the passage, not to mention the frustration it causes. Then, when **writing**, they have to create ideas and organize them into meaningful phrases, clauses and sentences that others can understand. **Writing** also requires proper punctuation, grammar and spelling. In order to use these essential skills, an acceptable level of vocabulary is needed. When **listening**, students have to pay attention to the words and try to interpret the meanings. Often, this involves several processes happening at once. Finally, when **speaking**, students have to think ahead about how to respond appropriately in conversations. This chart asks students to answer yes or no to these questions.

Rate Yourself

Rate yourself on how you feel about your own English vocabulary. Answer yes or no.

Yes	No	
		Frequently, I encounter words that I cannot pronounce or do not understand.
		Repeating new words and using a dictionary or thesaurus helps improve my vocabulary.
		When my teacher uses pictures, flash cards and other activities, I feel like I am learning new words more easily.
		Using a dictionary helps me to understand new words. It also helps me to see how words are pronounced and broken down into syllables.
		Reading introduces me to new words and helps improve my vocabulary.

OTM18112 ISBN: 9781770788718 © On The Mark Press

Repetition is Important!

In order to understand new words, it is important to learn and use them. This workbook presents vocabulary words in a repetitious manner and in different contexts. This framework provides an opportunity to use repetition, which is the key. By learning the meanings of words and interacting with them in different ways, students begin to feel more comfortable using the words. After completing a lesson, the words soon become a larger part of the learner's language.

Using the Dictionary and Thesaurus

It is important to use a good dictionary and thesaurus while reading; these tools should be on hand at all times and used when needed. Also, it is very important that the dictionary or thesaurus match the level at which the student is learning-bookstores carry these resource books at various levels and the right level must be chosen. Digital tools are very useful for everyday conversations as they are easily accessible and put students more at ease. Using a dictionary or thesaurus can mean the difference between understanding and not understanding a passage or a conversation. Having these tools on hand makes it possible to look up the word and its meaning immediately without having to wait until later. It is very important that students look up the words themselves rather than relying upon a teacher or another person to explain the meanings to them. In that way, they remember them better. Furthermore, while writing, dictionaries and thesauruses help quickly to improve word choice and to raise vocabulary to a higher level.

Keeping a Personal Dictionary

A personal dictionary can be an easy, invaluable tool in learning new words. It is simply a list of unfamiliar words and their meanings written into a notebook or recorded on the computer. When learning new vocabulary, it is important to write down new words encountered while reading or speaking, look them up in a dictionary or thesaurus and organize them in a meaningful way. Grouping words according to root words, prefixes and suffixes is one useful way of learning new words. By adding words to lists and reviewing the formats on a regular basis, learners become more familiar with the way in which patterns interact to help them become more successful at using vocabulary.

Flash Cards Can Help

Flash Cards are an excellent way to learn new vocabulary: making and using flashcards is a fast, efficient way to learn new vocabulary. The new word goes on one side and the meaning goes on the other side—together they form a useful way to record, practise and learn new vocabulary. Writing a sentence to accompany the words helps, and it is easy to review the cards as part of daily routines: on the bus, during lunch breaks, etc.

Find Mentors or Other Helpers!

It is very important to practise new skills every day, and it does not have to happen alone. Finding a learning partner or mentor is an ideal way to practise vocabulary and build confidence. Also, when learners are given opportunities in class to interact with each other in this way learning happens even more easily. If needed, tutors can help as well. There are several other ways to build vocabulary such as volunteering for organizations and businesses at jobs that require conversation. These methods quickly provide rewards in learning and take place in a natural setting. They provide the learner with valuable opportunities to use the English language to improve speaking, and enhance vocabulary. Public libraries frequently offer conversation classes, as well, in which people can simply get together with others to practise English.

Practising Clear Speech

There are many ways to practise pronunciation, and it is important to recognize that clear speech is extremely important. At home, reading aloud and recording articles from text or online sources and reviewing the recordings to make changes helps learners speak more effectively. Online websites are great places to learn more effective speech through listening and practising important sounds and phrases. It is a great way to learn alone or in groups. Some websites are very advanced and allow students to listen, read, record, receive feedback and practise in unique ways.

Reading For Thirty Minutes Daily Is Essential

One of the most effective ways to learn new vocabulary is by reading regularly, and frequently. Busy students benefit by setting aside thirty minutes at the end of the day for reading. The internet is the preferred method of reading today, and there are several websites with reading material geared to teaching new vocabulary. These websites contain a variety of formats including novels, short stories, poems, news articles, etc. Moreover, tackling new information while learning is also beneficial.

OTM18112   ISBN: 9781770788718 © On The Mark Press

Summarizing and paraphrasing the main ideas and key points while reading helps tremendously. By setting aside a short period of time each day to read, learners will soon begin to reap the benefits.

Syllabication

The vowels are **a, e, i, o** and **u**. Sometimes, **y** and **w** are also considered vowel sounds. Syllables are the sounds heard when these words are pronounced, and they contain separate sounds. The number of syllables in a word is the number of times the listener hears a vowel sound. For example, in the word **dog**, there is one syllable—the sound of the short vowel **o**. In the word **puppy,** there are two syllables—the sound of the short vowel **u** and the sound of the vowel sound **y** (pronounced **long- e**). Dictionaries separate words into syllables using hyphens or dots. Dividing new words into syllables while reading is a helpful exercise not to be overlooked. It is amazing how quickly new words can become part of everyday vocabulary by practising this activity.

To Divide Words into Syllables:

- Divide words after prefixes: un-clean;
- Divide words before suffixes: express-ing;
- Divide words between double consonants: fos-sil;
- For words with long vowel sounds, divide after the vowel: slo-gan;
- For words with short vowel sounds: divide after the consonant: sev-en.

Prefixes/ Suffixes/Root Words

Prefixes

Prefixes are letters or groups of letters added to the beginnings of words; they change the meanings of the words. Common prefixes are **re, ex,** and **pre**. For example, learners probably use the word **redo** frequently. What does **redo** mean? By breaking the word into syllables, it can be seen that **do** means to perform an activity. By adding the prefix **re**, which means **to do again**, the meaning changes. It is evident that knowing the meaning of a prefix and the root word, can help in figuring out the meanings of many new words. Other widely used prefixes include **un, in** and **dis**.

Suffixes

Suffixes are letters or groups of letters that appear at the endings of words. Like prefixes, suffixes change the meanings of words. Furthermore, as a suffix is added to a word, the word changes from one format or part of speech to another. For example, the suffix **ment** means a state of being or particular place. By adding **ment** to the verb establish, the word establishment results, which means a location where people carry out different procedures. Common suffixes include **ment, tion, ly**. By taking time to break words down into words and suffixes, they are easier to learn, use and remember.

Root Words

Root words are the main or basic parts of words, and these basic parts contain the meanings of the words. For example, the root word **care** means having or showing concern. Other words develop from this basic word such as careful, careless and carefully. Sometimes, words contain more than one root word such as popcorn (pop and corn) and fireman (fire and man). Since root words contain the meanings of words, it is important to use these roots to help unlock the meaning of other words. Students will be amazed at the number of words they can add to their vocabularies by studying root words and their meanings. Grammar books and online sources often contain lists of root words and their meanings that help learners acquire this skill. It quickly helps with the identification of the meanings of many words and recognizes the relationships with other languages, as well.

Learning Words From Context

Using context means using words and sentences situated **close to the sentence in question** to decipher the meaning of a word or expression. By examining the nearby words and sentences, it is possible to figure out the meaning of new words as well as entire sentences. A good strategy is to read through the entire sentence and search for the key words as they are good clues to meaning. Another strategy is to read the sentences before and after the sentence or phrase in question as they also contain meaningful clues. These clues are called context clues. It is good practise to read back at least two sentences and forward at least one sentence while searching for clues.

 Now let's practise. Look through this sentence to find the key words as they contain valuable clues to the meaning. Read this sentence. **After paying off all of their credit cards, the young couple felt like a tremendous load had been taken off their shoulders.** By determining the meaning of the word, **tremendous** (massive, huge, monumental), it is possible to see that the sentence means that the young couple feel that the pressure of the credit cards no longer exists.

 OTM18112   ISBN: 9781770788718 © On The Mark Press

Summary:

- Repetition is important, so practise words in different ways.
- Carry and use a dictionary and thesaurus (print or online).
- Make and use flash cards and a personal dictionary.
- Regularly practise clear speech.
- Read on a daily basis.
- Study format: Divide words into syllables, locate root words, prefixes and suffixes of words.

Follow these steps for each lesson.

1. **REPETITION:** Repeat the word aloud several times.

2. **READ:** Read the vocabulary words and definitions.

3. **MATCH:** Match the new word or sentence to the picture.

4. **PERSONAL DICTIONARY:** Create your own personal dictionary. On each page, include:

   a. A dictionary definition

   b. A sample sentence

   c. An original sentence

5. **READ:** Read daily for at least 30 minutes.

6. **PRACTISE:** Examine prefixes, suffixes, and root words, of words and find new words that contain the same patterns.

9. **CONTEXT:** Use context clues to help you learn new words.

10. **DICTIONARY and THESAURUS:** Keep these tools handy, and use them frequently.

OTM18112   ISBN: 9781770788718 © On The Mark Press

Lesson 1: Personal Information

Read the vocabulary words and meanings aloud. Look at the illustrations and follow the strategies listed on page 12. Try using the word in a sentence out loud.

	Vocabulary Word and Meaning	Illustration
1	**first name** The word by which a person is called.	Narinder
2	**middle initial** The first letter of a person's middle name.	J
3	**surname** A person's last name.	Singh
4	**address** The location at which a person can be contacted.	N. Singh 545 Maple Street, Toronto, ON, L1H 1J3
5	**Social Insurance Number** A number issued by the Canadian government that authorizes a person to work in Canada.	
6	**E-mail address** A location on the computer to send or receive electronic mail.	narinder@gmail.com
7	**Dependents** Persons such as children or others who depend upon someone else for support.	

8 **Town/City**
A settled area where people live or work.

9 **Country**
An area or region ruled by one central government.

10 **Home phone number**
Phone number at home.

11 **Business phone number**
Phone number at a place of business.

N. Singh

545 Maple Street,
Toronto, ON, L1H 1J3
123-456-7890

12 **Street**
A road for travelling from place to place.

13 **Avenue**
A street with houses on both sides.

OTM18112 ISBN: 9781770788718 © On The Mark Press

14   **Spell**
        To say or write the letters in the order that they
        make up a word.

15   **Birthdate**
        The day, month and year of a person's birth.

16   **Cell phone number**
        A person's mobile phone number.

Zeynep Demir/Shutterstock.com

17   **Voicemail**
        Recorded messages that can be replayed.

18   **Province**
        An area or region of a country containing its
        own government in charge of certain services.

19   **Sex/gender**
        Being male or female.

20   **Postal code**   L1H 1J3
        A system of six numbers and letters assigned to
        specific areas of Canada.

Matching Vocabulary Words

first name	middle initial	surname	address
dependents	town/city	spell	
country	business phone number	postal code	

Match the illustrations with the vocabulary word. Write the name from the list above beside the picture.

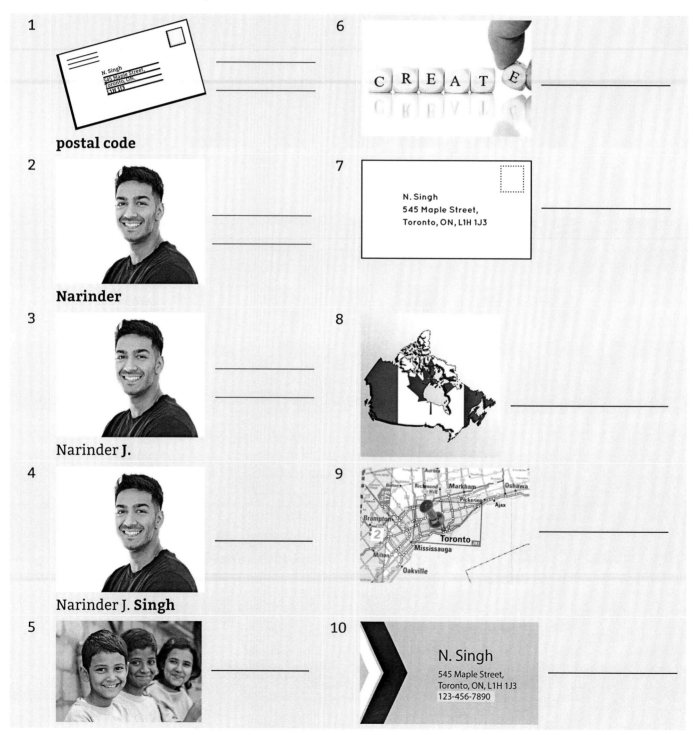

1.   **postal code**

2.   **Narinder**

3.   Narinder **J.**

4.   Narinder J. **Singh**

5.

6.

7.

8.

9.

10.

OTM18112   ISBN: 9781770788718 © On The Mark Press

Matching Vocabulary Words

social insurance number   home phone number   street
avenue   province   cell phone number
birthdate   sex/gender   voicemail
email address

11

_____
_____

16

_____

12

_____

17

_____

Zeynep Demir/Shutterstock.com

13

_____

18

_____

14

_____

19

_____

15

_____

20

_____

Matching Sentences and Illustrations

On the next page write the sentence on the line that matches the illustration.

Pay attention to the **boldfaced** word.

a) Is your **first name** Narinder?

b) My **middle initial** is J.

c) Our **surname** is Singh.

d) I forgot to write my **address** at the top of the page.

e) You cannot work in Canada without a **Social Insurance Number**.

f) Can I please have your **E-mail address**.

g) My mom listed my brother and I as her **dependents**.

h) There are many advantages to living in a **town/city**.

i) Which flag represents your **country**?

j) I need your **home phone number** so I can call you tonight.

k) Is your **business phone number** on your business card?

l) That **street** is not very busy anymore.

m) The houses on that **avenue** have some lovely porches.

n) Make sure you can **spell** all the words in this lesson.

o) The form was returned because it was missing the **birthdate**.

p) My friend purchased a new **cell phone** today.

q) Did you get the message I left on your **voicemail**?

r) Is your home province British Columbia?

s) The form asks you to indicate your **sex/gender**.

t) **A postal code** in Canada contains three letters and three numbers.

OTM18112 ISBN: 9781770788718 © On The Mark Press

Matching Sentences and Illustrations

Read the sentences on page 18 and write the sentence on the line that matches the illustration.

Pay attention to the **boldfaced** word.

	Sentence	Illustration
1		**postal code**
2		**Narinder**
3		
4		
5		

OTM18112   ISBN: 9781770788718 © On The Mark Press

6 _____
   _____
   _____

N. Singh
545 Maple Street,
Toronto, ON, L1H 1J3
123-456-7890

7 _____
   _____
   _____

Narinder **J.** Singh

8 _____
   _____
   _____

Narinder J. **Singh**

9 _____
   _____
   _____

10 _____
   _____
   _____

11 _____
   _____
   _____

12 _____
   _____
   _____

13 _____
_____

14 _____
_____

narinder@gmail.com

15 _____
_____

16 _____
_____

2013 01 NOV

17 _____
_____

Voice Mail

18 _____
_____

Zeynep Demir/
Shutterstock.com

19 _____
_____

20 _____
_____

Lesson 2: Family Information

Read the vocabulary words and meanings aloud. Look at the illustrations and follow the strategies listed on page 12. Try using the word in a sentence out loud.

	Vocabulary Words/Meanings	Illustration
1	**Family** A group of people, usually related, who may live together.	
2	**Siblings** Brothers or sisters	
3	**Grandparents** The parents of a person's father or mother.	
4	**Aunt** The sister of a person's parents.	
5	**Parents** A person's father and mother.	

OTM18112   ISBN: 9781770788718 © On The Mark Press

Read the vocabulary words and meanings aloud. Look at the illustrations and follow the strategies listed on page 12. Try using the word in a sentence out loud.

	Vocabulary Words/Meanings	Illustration
6	**Granddaughter** The daughter of a person's son or daughter.	
7	**Grandson** The son of a person's son or daughter.	
8	**Grandmother** The mother of a person's father or mother.	
9	**Members** People belonging to a group.	
10	**Uncle** The brother of one's father or mother.	

Read the vocabulary words and meanings aloud. Look at the illustrations and follow the strategies listed on page 12. Try using the word in a sentence out loud.

Vocabulary Words/Meanings	Illustration
11 **Nephew** The son of a person's brother or sister.	
12 **Father** A person's male parent.	
13 **Mother** A person's female parent.	
14 **Grandfather** The father of a person's father or mother.	
15 **Sister** A female person with whom one shares one or both parents.	

OTM18112   ISBN: 9781770788718 © On The Mark Press

Name:

Read the vocabulary words and meanings aloud. Look at the illustrations and follow the strategies listed on page 12. Try using the word in a sentence out loud.

	Vocabulary Words/Meanings	Illustration
16	**Brother** A male person with whom one shares one or both parents.	
17	**Niece** The daughter of a person's brother or sister.	
18	**Children** Young males or females who have not yet become adults.	
19	**Son** A person's male child.	
20	**Daughter** A person's female child.	

Matching Vocabulary Words

grandmother	members	grandson	brother
father	grandfather	siblings	
family	granddaughter	nephew	

Match the illustrations with the vocabulary word. Write the name from the list beside the picture.

1 _____

2 _____

3 _____

4 _____

5 _____

6 _____

7 _____

8 _____

9 _____

10 _____

OTM18112 ISBN: 9781770788718 © On The Mark Press

Matching Vocabulary Words

niece	son	mother	aunt
grandparents	parents	uncle	
sister	daughter	children	

Match the illustrations with the vocabulary word. Write the name from the list beside the picture on the line.

11  _____

16  _____

12  _____

17  _____

13  _____

18  _____

14  _____

19  _____

15  _____

20  _____

OTM18112   ISBN: 9781770788718 © On The Mark Press

Matching Sentences and Illustrations

On the next page write the number of the sentence on the line that matches the illustration.

Pay attention to the **boldfaced** word.

a) Our **family** always has a picnic on Canada Day.

b) Both **siblings** attended the assembly at the school.

c) Do your **grandparents** still live on this street?

d) **Aunt** May is my father's oldest sister.

e) Do your **parents** take a holiday every summer?

f) Which school does your **granddaughter** attend?

g) Paul's **grandson** plays hockey tonight at the arena.

h) Where was your **grandmother** born?

i) We met all **members** of my father's family this summer in China.

j) **Uncle** Bill is my father's only brother.

k) Where does your **nephew** play badminton?

l) Our **father** is coming to see the play tonight.

m) Does your **mother** always take the train to work?

n) My **grandfather** turned sixty last month.

o) My **sister** and I learned how to fish for clams this summer in Victoria.

p) This picture of my youngest **brother** was taken at his school.

q) My **niece** just left on a tour of Europe.

r) There were over forty **children** on the bus this morning.

s) Does your **son** live in the high-rise condo on this street?

t) Please ask your **daughte**r for that delicious recipe.

OTM18112   ISBN: 9781770788718 © On The Mark Press

Matching Sentences and Illustrations

Read the sentences on page 28 and write the number of the sentence on the line that matches the illustration.

Pay attention to the **boldfaced** word.

1 _____

6 _____

2 _____

7 _____

3 _____

8 _____

4 _____

9 _____

5 _____

10 _____

OTM18112   ISBN: 9781770788718 © On The Mark Press

Matching Sentences and Illustrations

Read the sentences on page 28 and write the number of the sentence on the line that matches the illustration.

Pay attention to the **boldfaced** word.

11 _____

16 _____

12 _____

17 _____

13 _____

18 _____

14 _____

19 _____

15 _____

20 _____

OTM18112   ISBN: 9781770788718 © On The Mark Press

Lesson 3: Numbers

Read the vocabulary words and meanings aloud. Look at the illustrations and follow the strategies listed on page 12. Try using the word in a sentence out loud.

	Vocabulary Words/Meanings	Illustration
1	**One** A single unit.	
2	**Two** The number that comes after one and before three.	
3	**Three** The number that comes after two and before four.	
4	**Four** The number that comes after three and before five.	
5	**Five** The number that comes after four and before six.	
6	**Six** The number that comes after five and before seven.	
7	**Seven** The number that comes after six and before eight.	
8	**Eight** The number that comes after seven and before nine.	
9	**Nine** The number that comes after eight and before ten.	
10	**Ten** The number that comes after nine and before eleven.	

OTM18112   ISBN: 9781770788718 © On The Mark Press

Read the vocabulary words and meanings aloud. Look at the illustrations and follow the strategies listed on page 12. Try using the word in a sentence out loud.

	Vocabulary Words/Meanings	Illustration
11	**First** The number that comes before any other number.	
12	**Second** The number that comes after first.	
13	**Third** The number that comes after second.	
14	**Fourth** The number that comes after third.	
15	**Fifth** The number that comes after fourth.	

OTM18112   ISBN: 9781770788718 © On The Mark Press

Read the vocabulary words and meanings aloud. Look at the illustrations and follow the strategies listed on page 12. Try using the word in a sentence out loud.

	Vocabulary Words/Meanings	Illustration
16	**Sixth** The number that comes after fifth.	
17	**Seventh** The number that comes after sixth.	
18	**Eighth** The number that comes after seventh.	
19	**Ninth** The number that comes after eighth.	
20	**Tenth** The number that comes after ninth.	

Matching Vocabulary Words

one	two	three	four	five
six	seven	eight	nine	ten
first	second	third	fourth	fifth
sixth	seventh	eighth	ninth	tenth

Match the illustrations with the vocabulary word. Write the number from the list above beside the picture.

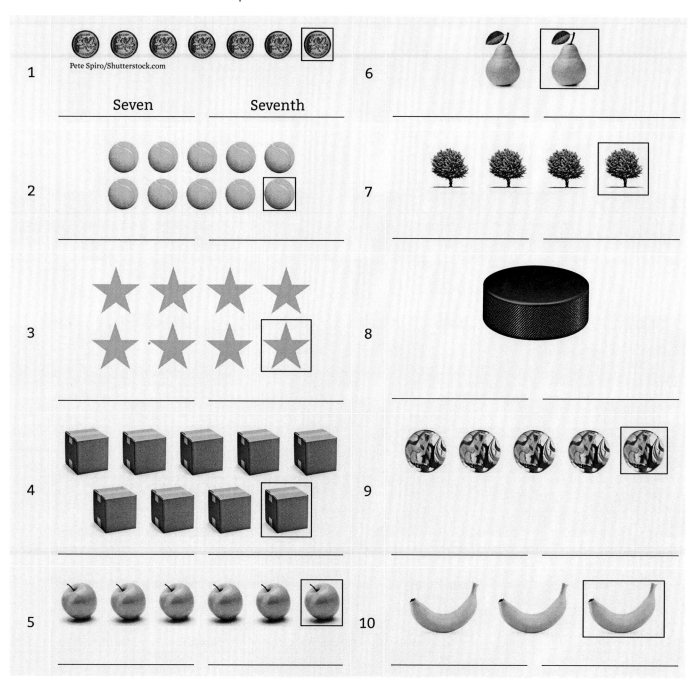

1　Pete Spiro/Shutterstock.com

　Seven　　　Seventh

2

3

4

5

6

7

8

9

10

OTM18112　ISBN: 9781770788718 © On The Mark Press

Matching Sentences and Illustrations

On the next page write the sentence on the line that matches the illustration.

Pay attention to the **boldfaced** word.

a)   There is only **one** apple in the bowl now.

b)   There are **two** puppies in the cage.

c)   The **three** cars were damaged in the crash.

d)   We asked **four** doctors for their opinions.

e)   My sister found **five** nickels in the park.

f)   The play begins at **six** o'clock.

g)   There were **seven** people at the conference.

h)   **Eight** people went on the city bus tour.

i)   **Nine** stores closed in that mall.

j)   All **ten** pennies were new and shiny.

k)   He was the **first** student to arrive this morning.

l)   Did you win **second** prize today?

m) She was the **third** person to join the group.

n)   I ate one **fourth** of the pumpkin pie.

o)   The movie was about the **fifth** prime minister of Canada.

p)   The match lasted until the **sixth** round.

q)   You answered the phone on the **seventh** ring.

r)   The **eighth** message faded out.

s)   He struck out in the **ninth** inning.

t)   The game ended after I scored the **tenth** goal.

OTM18112   ISBN: 9781770788718 © On The Mark Press

Matching Sentences and Illustrations

Read the sentences on page 35 and write the sentence on the line that matches the illustration.

Pay attention to the **boldfaced** word.

1 _____

2 _____

3 _____

4 _____

5 _____

6 _____

7 _____

8 _____

9 _____

10 _____

OTM18112   ISBN: 9781770788718 © On The Mark Press

Matching Sentences and Illustrations

Read the sentences on page 35 and write the sentence on the line that matches the illustration.

Pay attention to the **boldfaced** word.

11 _____

16 _____

12 _____

17 _____

13 _____

18 _____

14 _____

19 _____

Pete Spiro/Shutterstock.com

15 _____

20 _____

OTM18112   ISBN: 9781770788718 © On The Mark Press

Lesson 4: Colours and Seasons

Read the vocabulary words and meanings aloud. Look at the illustrations and follow the strategies listed on page 12. Try using the word in a sentence out loud.

	Vocabulary Words/Meanings	Illustration
1	**Black** The darkest colour.	
2	**White** The lightest or palest colour.	
3	**Grey** A colour that is a combination of black and white.	
4	**Silver** A metallic-looking light grey colour.	
5	**Gold** A metallic-looking dark yellow colour.	

OTM18112   ISBN: 9781770788718 © On The Mark Press

Read the vocabulary words and meanings aloud. Look at the illustrations and follow the strategies listed on page 12. Try using the word in a sentence out loud.

	Vocabulary Words/Meanings	Illustration
6	**Red** A colour that looks like a cherry.	
7	**Blue** A colour that looks like the sky.	
8	**Green** A colour that looks like trees or shrubs.	
9	**Orange** A colour that looks like a combination of red and yellow.	
10	**Purple** A colour that looks like a combination of red and blue.	

Read the vocabulary words and meanings aloud. Look at the illustrations and follow the strategies listed on page 12. Try using the word in a sentence out loud.

	Vocabulary Words/Meanings	Illustration
11	**Beige** A very light brown colour.	
12	**Pink** A colour that looks like pale red.	
13	**Fuchsia** A colour that looks like a combination of red and purple.	
14	**Turquoise** A colour that looks like a combination of blue and green.	
15	**Charcoal** A colour that looks like black and grey.	

OTM18112 ISBN: 9781770788718 © On The Mark Press

Read the vocabulary words and meanings aloud. Look at the illustrations and follow the strategies listed on page 12. Try using the word in a sentence out loud.

	Vocabulary Words/Meanings	Illustration
16	**Spring** The season between winter and summer.	
17	**Summer** The season between spring and fall.	
18	**Fall** The season between summer and winter.	
19	**Autumn** Another name for fall.	
20	**Winter** The cold season between autumn and spring.	

Matching Vocabulary Words

blue	grey	autumn	winter	fall
spring	fuchsia	green	black	gold

Match the illustrations with the vocabulary word. Write the name from the list above beside the picture.

1 _____

2 _____

3 _____

4 _____

5 _____

6 _____

7 _____

8 _____

9 _____

10 _____

OTM18112 ISBN: 9781770788718 © On The Mark Press

Matching Vocabulary Words

turquoise   summer   purple   orange   silver
pink   charcoal   white   beige   red

Match the illustrations with the vocabulary word. Write the name from the list above beside the picture.

11 _____

16 _____

Jackey/Shutterstock.com

12 _____

17 _____

13 _____

18 _____

14 _____

19 _____

15 _____

20 _____

Matching Sentences and Illustrations

On the next page write the number of the sentence on the line that matches the illustration.

Pay attention to the **boldfaced** word.

a) Two **black** cats ran across the road.

b) Mother sewed buttons on my **white** coat.

c) After it rained, the sky was still **grey**.

d) Mom's hair is turning a beautiful shade of **silver**.

e) My sister wore a **gold** dress to the wedding.

f) The **red** bow fell off the gift.

g) Those **blue** towels are still wet.

h) The forest still looks fresh and **green**.

i) Are you wearing **orange** at Halloween?

j) My father loves **purple** plums and grapes.

k) Our bathroom feels calmer since we painted it **beige**.

l) My cheeks turned **pink** when I went out into the cold.

m) I was the only person wearing **fuchsia**.

n) Dad combined blue and green paint to make **turquoise**.

o) I thought my sweater was black, but it is **charcoal**.

p) We plant tulips every **spring**.

q) When do you think **summer** will end?

r) The **fall** colors in Quebec were breathtaking.

s) The birds head south during the **autumn**.

t) Are you going skiing this **winter**?

OTM18112   ISBN: 9781770788718 © On The Mark Press

Matching Sentences and Illustrations

Read the sentences on page 44 and write the number of the sentence on the line that matches the illustration.

Pay attention to the **boldfaced** word.

1 _____

2 _____

3 _____

4 _____

5 _____

6 _____

7 _____

8 _____

9 _____

10 _____

Name:

Matching Sentences and Illustrations

Read the sentences on page 44 and write the number of the sentence on the line that matches the illustration.

Pay attention to the **boldfaced** word.

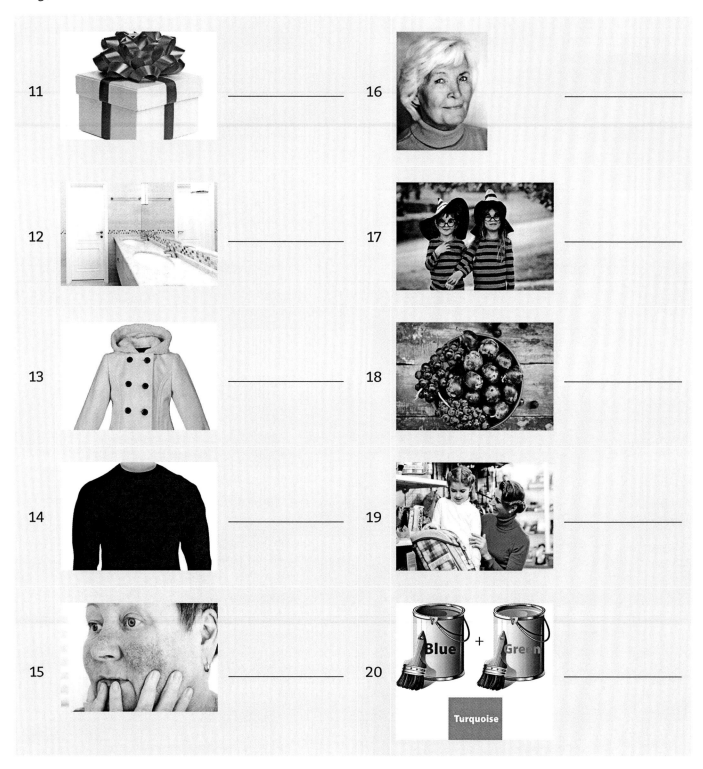

11 _____

16 _____

12 _____

17 _____

13 _____

18 _____

14 _____

19 _____

15 _____

20 _____

   OTM18112   ISBN: 9781770788718 © On The Mark Press

Lesson 5: Telling Time

Read the vocabulary words and meanings aloud. Look at the illustrations and follow the strategies listed on page 12. Try using the word in a sentence out loud.

	Vocabulary Words/Meanings	Illustration
1	**One o'clock** One hour past noon or midnight.	
2	**Two fifteen** Fifteen minutes past two.	
3	**Three thirty** Thirty minutes past three.	
4	**Three forty-five** Forty-five minutes past three or a quarter to four.	
5	**Five-after-five** Five minutes past five or five oh five.	

Read the vocabulary words and meanings aloud. Look at the illustrations and follow the strategies listed on page 12. Try using the word in a sentence out loud.

	Vocabulary Words/Meanings	Illustration
6	**Six twenty-five** Twenty-five minutes past six or six twenty-five.	
7	**Midnight** Twelve o'clock a.m.	
8	**Noon** Twelve o'clock p.m.	
9	**Seven a.m.** Seven o'clock in the morning.	
10	**Eight p.m.** Eight o'clock at night.	

OTM18112 ISBN: 9781770788718 © On The Mark Press

Read the vocabulary words and meanings aloud. Look at the illustrations and follow the strategies listed on page 12. Try using the word in a sentence out loud.

	Vocabulary Words/Meanings	Illustration
11	**Ten after nine** Ten minutes after nine or nine ten.	
12	**Morning** The time between midnight and noon.	
13	**Evening** The latter part of the day until the early part of the night.	
14	**Today** This day.	
15	**Yesterday** The day before today.	

Read the vocabulary words and meanings aloud. Look at the illustrations and follow the strategies listed on page 12. Try using the word in a sentence out loud.

	Vocabulary Words/Meanings	Illustration
16	**Tomorrow** The day after today.	
17	**Tonight** This night.	
18	**Last night** The night before this one.	
19	**This week** The present week.	
20	**Next week** The week after this one.	

OTM18112 ISBN: 9781770788718 © On The Mark Press

Matching Vocabulary Words

Three Thirty	Ten After Nine	Eight P.M.	Noon	This Week
Tonight	One O'Clock	Two Fifteen	Evening	Six Twenty

Match the illustrations with the vocabulary word. Write the name from the list above beside the picture.

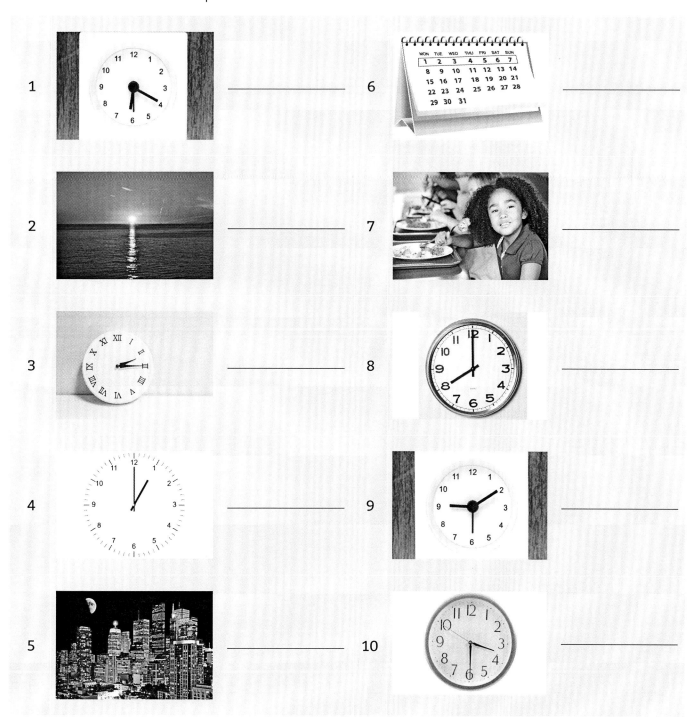

Matching Vocabulary Words

Four Forty-Five	Next Week	Seven A.M.	Tomorrow	Five to Five
Morning	Yesterday	Midnight	Today	Last Night

Match the illustrations with the vocabulary word. Write the name from the list above beside the picture.

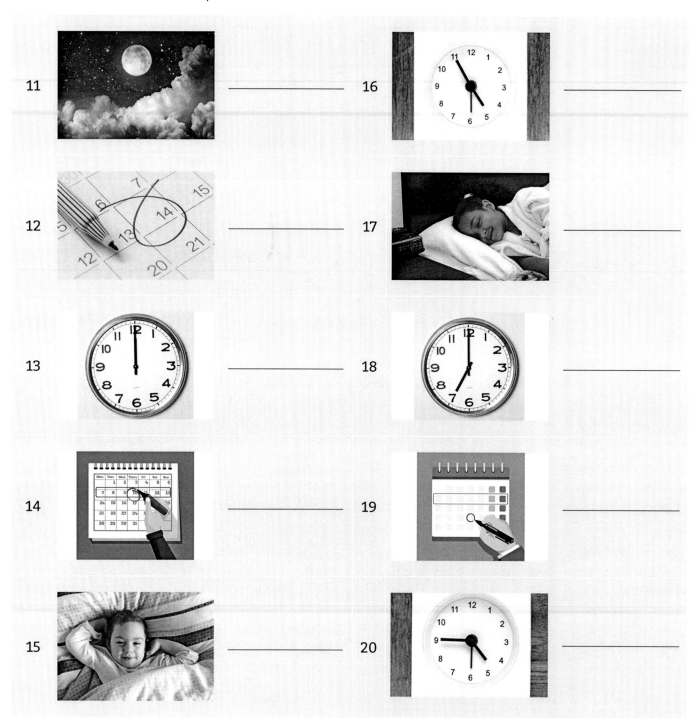

11 _____

16 _____

12 _____

17 _____

13 _____

18 _____

14 _____

19 _____

15 _____

20 _____

OTM18112   ISBN: 9781770788718 © On The Mark Press

Matching Sentences and Illustrations

On the next page write the sentence on the line that matches the illustration.

Pay attention to the **boldfaced** word.

a) Does your lunch break end at **one o'clock** today?

b) My dentist appointment is at **two fifteen**.

c) The school bell rang at **three thirty**.

d) Meet me at the swimming pool at **four forty-five**.

e) The basketball team arrives at **five-after-five**.

f) Usually the doors open for the play at **six twenty-five**.

g) I studied until **midnight** last night.

h) The car will be ready at **noon**.

i) I have to catch the plane at **seven am**.

j) After the long trip, the children fell asleep before **eight pm**.

k) The chemistry class begins at **ten after nine**.

l) Ellie had cereal for breakfast this **morning**.

m) It was a peaceful **evening** at the lake.

n) I went out for lunch **today.**

o) Registration for the piano course ended **yesterday**.

p) Are you going to the gym **tomorrow**?

q) That street was busy **tonight**.

r) We invited visitors to our house to watch a movie **last night**.

s) There is no science class **this week**.

t) The shipment will arrive **next week**?

Matching Sentences and Illustrations

Read the sentences on page 53 and write the sentence on the line that matches the illustration.

Pay attention to the **boldfaced** word.

1 _____

2 _____

3 _____

4 _____

5 _____

6 _____

7 _____

8 _____

9 _____

10 _____

OTM18112   ISBN: 9781770788718 © On The Mark Press

Matching Sentences and Illustrations

Read the sentences on page 53 and write the sentence on the line that matches the illustration.

Pay attention to the **boldfaced** word.

11 _____

16 _____

12 _____

17 _____

13 _____

18 _____

14 _____

19 _____

15 _____

20 _____

Lesson 6: Community Locations

Read the vocabulary words and meanings out loud. Look at the illustrations and follow the strategies listed on page 12. Try using the word in a sentence out loud.

Vocabulary Words/Meanings	Illustration
1 **Library** A public building where people borrow books, read or study.	
2 **Bank** A place where people deposit, withdraw and manage their money.	JHVEPhoto/Shutterstock.com
3 **Drug store** A store where medicines and other products are sold.	
4 **Bus stop** A place where passengers wait for the bus.	
5 **Restaurant** A public place for ordering and eating meals.	

OTM18112   ISBN: 9781770788718 © On The Mark Press

Read the vocabulary words and meanings out loud. Look at the illustrations and follow the strategies listed on page 12. Try using the word in a sentence out loud.

	Vocabulary Words/Meanings	Illustration
6	**Grocery store** A store that sells food and household products.	
7	**Insurance office** A place where customers buy home and automobile insurance protection in case damage occurs.	
8	**Convenience store** A small store where customers can purchase products quickly without waiting in long lines.	
9	**Airport** A place where people go to get on an airplane.	
10	**Office supplies store** A store that sells paper, pencils, and other office supplies.	

Read the vocabulary words and meanings out loud. Look at the illustrations and follow the strategies listed on page 12. Try using the word in a sentence out loud.

	Vocabulary Words/Meanings	Illustration
11	**Gas station** A place that sells gasoline or other products for motor vehicles.	
12	**Dry cleaners** A place where people take their clothes to be chemically cleaned.	
13	**Shopping mall** A large building with many stores sometimes on several floors.	
14	**Medical clinic** A place to receive medical assistance from a doctor.	
15	**Hairdresser** A person who cuts, colours and styles hair.	

OTM18112 ISBN: 9781770788718 © On The Mark Press

Read the vocabulary words and meanings out loud. Look at the illustrations and follow the strategies listed on page 12. Try using the word in a sentence out loud.

Vocabulary Words/Meanings	Illustration
16 **Electronics store** A store that sells phones, computers, televisions and other products.	
17 **Hospital** A place where sick and injured people receive treatment for illnesses or diseases.	
18 **Train station** A place where people go to get on a train.	
19 **Place of worship** A building where people go to worship God and pray.	
20 **School** A building where students learn at different grade levels.	

Matching Vocabulary Words

grocery store   hairdresser   hospital   school   restaurant

library   drug store   gas station   shopping mall   airport

Match the illustrations with the vocabulary word. Write the name from the list above beside the picture.

1  _____

6  _____

2  _____

7  _____

3  _____

8  _____

4  _____

9  _____

5  _____

10  _____

OTM18112   ISBN: 9781770788718 © On The Mark Press

Matching Vocabulary Words

electronics store   place of worship   dry cleaners   bank

insurance office   medical clinic   train station   bus stop

office supplies store   convenience store

Match the illustrations with the vocabulary word. Write the name from the list above beside the picture.

11 _____

16 _____

12 _____

17 _____

13 _____

18 _____

14 _____

19 _____

15 _____

20 _____

Matching Sentences and Illustrations

On the next page write the number of the sentence on the line that matches the illustration. Pay attention to the **boldfaced** word.

a)   The **library** clerk called about overdue books.

b)   Who did you speak to at the **bank** about the deposit?

c)   Wait for me at the entrance to the **drug store**.

d)   It was freezing at the **bus stop** this morning.

e)   Please meet me inside the **restaurant**.

f)   My father used the express line at the **grocery store**.

g)   I forgot to call the **insurance office** about the accident.

h)   The **convenience store** across the street sells milk and bread.

i)   We were tired after walking through the **airport**.

j)   The **office supplies store** is next to the bank.

k)   Does the **gas station** on the corner offer car wash coupons?

l)   The **dry cleaners** ruined my white shirt.

m)   Please take my sister with you to the **shopping mall**.

n)   Does that **medical clinic** open at noon?

o)   How long has your **hairdresser** been cutting your hair?

p)   The phones at that **electronics store** are selling out quickly.

q)   Will the **hospital** call about your surgery?

r)   That **train station** is the busiest spot in the city.

s)   Are you still looking for a **place of worship**?

t)   There was a fire drill at that **school** this afternoon.

     OTM18112   ISBN: 9781770788718 © On The Mark Press

Matching Sentences and Illustrations

Read the sentences on page 62 and write the number of the sentence on the line that matches the illustration. Pay attention to the **boldfaced** word.

1 _____

2 _____

3 _____

4 _____

5 _____

6 _____

7 _____

8 _____

9 _____

10 _____

OTM18112   ISBN: 9781770788718 © On The Mark Press

Matching Sentences and Illustrations

Read the sentences on page 62 and write the number of the sentence on the line that matches the illustration. Pay attention to the **boldfaced** word.

11 _____

16 _____

12 _____

17 _____

13 _____

18 _____

14 _____

19 _____

15 _____

20 _____

OTM18112 ISBN: 9781770788718 © On The Mark Press

Lesson 7: At the Supermarket

Read the vocabulary words and meanings aloud. Look at the illustrations and follow the strategies listed on page 12. Try using the word in a sentence out loud.

	Vocabulary Words/Meanings	Illustration
1	**Customer** A person who purchases goods or services at a store or other place of business.	
2	**Clerk** A person who works in a store or business and performs various jobs.	
3	**Cashier** A person who takes payments for goods or services.	
4	**Shopping cart** A metal container on wheels used for carrying groceries or other items.	
5	**Label** A small piece of paper attached to an item that describes it and states the price.	

Read the vocabulary words and meanings aloud. Look at the illustrations and follow the strategies listed on page 12. Try using the word in a sentence out loud.

	Vocabulary Words/Meanings	Illustration
6	**Supermarket manager** The head employee in charge of a supermarket.	
7	**Produce manager** The head person in the vegetable and fruit section of a supermarket.	
8	**Meat manager** The head person in the meat department of a supermarket.	
9	**Aisle** A space between shelves in a supermarket where people walk and push their carts.	
10	**Checkout** A place people go to pay for their purchases.	

OTM18112 ISBN: 9781770788718 © On The Mark Press

Read the vocabulary words and meanings aloud. Look at the illustrations and follow the strategies listed on page 12. Try using the word in a sentence out loud.

	Vocabulary Words/Meanings	Illustration
11	**Self-checkout** A place where customers can operate a small machine to pay for their purchases.	
12	**Express checkout** A place to pay for a small number of items.	
13	**Customer service** A place to receive assistance in a store or place of business.	
14	**Shopping basket** A small portable container in which customers carry a small number of items.	
15	**Coupon** A piece of paper customers use to receive a discount.	

Read the vocabulary words and meanings aloud. Look at the illustrations and follow the strategies listed on page 12. Try using the word in a sentence out loud.

	Vocabulary Words/Meanings	Illustration
16	**Raincheck** A piece of paper detailing a discount and date to purchase an item that is on sale but out of stock.	
17	**Discount** An amount subtracted from the regular price.	
18	**Cash register** A machine used to calculate the amount of a sale or sale.	
19	**Conveyor belt** A flat movable surface where customers place items at a checkout.	
20	**Receipt** A piece of paper showing that a customer has paid for items.	

OTM18112 ISBN: 9781770788718 © On The Mark Press

Matching Vocabulary Words

clerk   express checkout   label   meat manager   cash register

aisle   self-checkout   customer   shopping cart   coupon

Match the illustrations with the vocabulary word. Write the name from the list above beside the picture.

1 _____

2 _____

3 _____

4 _____

5 _____

6 _____

7 _____

8 _____

9 _____

10 _____

Matching Vocabulary Words

shopping basket	produce manger	conveyor belt	rain-check
customer service	cashier	receipt	checkout
supermarket manager	discount		

Match the illustrations with the vocabulary word. Write the name from the list above beside the picture.

11 _____

16 _____

12 _____

17 _____

13 _____

18 _____

14 _____

19 _____

15 _____

20 _____

OTM18112   ISBN: 9781770788718 © On The Mark Press

Matching Sentences and Illustrations

On the next page write the number of the sentence on the line that matches the illustration. Pay attention to the **boldfaced** word.

a) The **customer** is selecting produce.

b) Does the **clerk** know when the sweet potatoes will arrive?

c) The **cashier** took my debit card to process the payment.

d) This **shopping cart** is very hard to steer.

e) I always read the food **label**.

f) The **supermarket manager** is talking to a staff member.

g) The **produce manager** is ordering bananas this week.

h) Ask the **meat manager** if turkeys are on sale tomorrow.

i) I couldn't find the jam in that **aisle**.

j) Take the groceries to the **checkout**.

k) The **self-checkout** is easy to operate.

l) My mother always uses the **express checkout** when she is in a hurry.

m) You can return the apples at the **customer service** counter.

n) Take a **shopping basket** because you only have a few items.

o) We cut out the **coupons** to save money.

p) The cashier gave me a **raincheck**, as they were out of the item on sale.

q) The lady received a **discount** or percentage off the item.

r) The **cash register** was left unattended.

s) The **conveyor belt** is moving slowly this morning.

t) I look over my **receipt** each time.

Matching Sentences and Illustrations

Read the sentences on page 71 and write the number of the sentence on the line that matches the illustration.

Pay attention to the **boldfaced** word.

1 _____   6 _____

2 _____   7 _____

3 _____   8 _____

4 _____   9 _____

5 _____   10 _____

OTM18112   ISBN: 9781770788718 © On The Mark Press

Matching Sentences and Illustrations

Read the sentences on page 71 and write the number of the sentence on the line that matches the illustration.

Pay attention to the **boldfaced** word.

Lesson 8: At the Bank

Read the vocabulary words and meanings aloud. Look at the illustrations and follow the strategies listed on page 12. Try using the word in a sentence out loud.

	Vocabulary Words/Meanings	Illustration
1	**Cash** Money in the form of bills or coins.	
2	**Cheque** A piece of paper ordering the bank to remove money from a person's account.	
3	**Chequing account** A bank account usually used for writing cheques.	
4	**Savings account** A bank account in which people save money.	
5	**Teller** A bank employee who assists customers.	

OTM18112 ISBN: 9781770788718 © On The Mark Press

Read the vocabulary words and meanings aloud. Look at the illustrations and follow the strategies listed on page 12. Try using the word in a sentence out loud.

	Vocabulary Words/Meanings	Illustration
6	**ATM machine** A computerized machine where customers make deposits and withdrawls.	
7	**Safe deposit box** Metal box for keeping securities safe, usually kept at the bank.	
8	**Chequebook** A book where customers keep cheques and record transactions.	
9	**Online banking** Banking that is carried out online.	
10	**E-transfer** A bank service allowing customers to transfer money online.	

Read the vocabulary words and meanings aloud. Look at the illustrations and follow the strategies listed on page 12. Try using the word in a sentence out loud.

	Vocabulary Words/Meanings	Illustration
11	**Deposit** To place funds in a bank account.	
12	**Currency** Another name for money.	
13	**Withdrawl** To remove money or funds from a bank account.	
14	**Bankbook** A book where customers record transactions.	
15	**Personal Identification Number (PIN)** A confidential number customers use for identification.	

OTM18112   ISBN: 9781770788718 © On The Mark Press

Read the vocabulary words and meanings aloud. Look at the illustrations and follow the strategies listed on page 12. Try using the word in a sentence out loud.

	Vocabulary Words/Meanings	Illustration
16	**Transfer** To removed funds from one account and deposit into another.	
17	**Debit card** A card linked to a person's bank account that customers use for making purchases.	
18	**Money order** A written order a person makes that tells the bank to pay money to a person or business.	
19	**Bank statement** A record of a person's bank transactions.	
20	**Credit card** A card issued by a bank that customers use for making purchases they pay for at a later date.	

Matching Vocabulary Words

chequebook   bank statement   teller   bankbook

money order   online banking   cash   withdrawl

ATM machine   chequing account

Match the illustrations with the vocabulary word. Write the name from the list above beside the picture.

1 _____

2 _____

3 _____

4 _____

5 _____

6 _____

7 _____

8 _____

9 _____

10 _____

OTM18112 ISBN: 9781770788718 © On The Mark Press

Matching Vocabulary Words

credit card   savings account   debit card   transfer

safe deposit box   currency   e-transfer   cheque

personal identification   deposit

number (PIN)

Match the illustrations with the vocabulary word. Write the name from the
list above beside the picture.

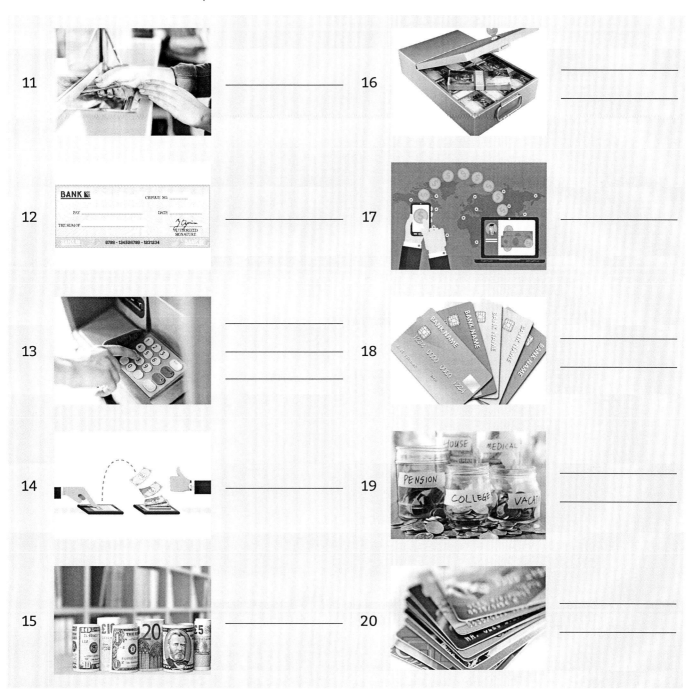

11 _____

12 _____

13 _____

14 _____

15 _____

16 _____

17 _____

18 _____

19 _____

20 _____

Matching Sentences and Illustrations

On the next page write the number of the sentence on the line that matches the illustration. Pay attention to the **boldfaced** word.

a) Some stores only take **cash** for payment.

b) Most of my customers pay me with a **cheque**.

c) How many bills did you pay with your **chequing account**?

d) To get a higher interest rate, you need to open a **savings account**.

e) The **teller** helped me send a wire transfer to India.

f) Don't go to the **ATM machine** alone at night.

g) Do you still keep your watches in a **safe deposit box**?

h) Don't forget to take your **chequebook**.

i) My mom uses **online banking** at work and at home.

j) The swimming pool will accept an **E-transfer** for the payment.

k) Are you making a **deposit** today?

l) When I visited Spain, I used a different **currency.**

m) Will you be making a **withdrawal** from your savings account this morning?

n) When I make a deposit, the teller gives me a printout in my **bankbook**.

o) Keep your **Personal Identification Number (PIN)** safe and secure.

p) **Transfer** money from your savings to your chequing account.

q) I pay for my groceries and gas using my **debit card.**

r) That company declined to accept my **money order**.

s) The **bank statement** contained an error concerning the date.

t) My brother used his **credit card** to pay for his new phone.

OTM18112   ISBN: 9781770788718 © On The Mark Press

Matching Sentences and Illustrations

Read the sentences on page 80 and write the number of the sentence on the line that matches the illustration.

Pay attention to the **boldfaced** word.

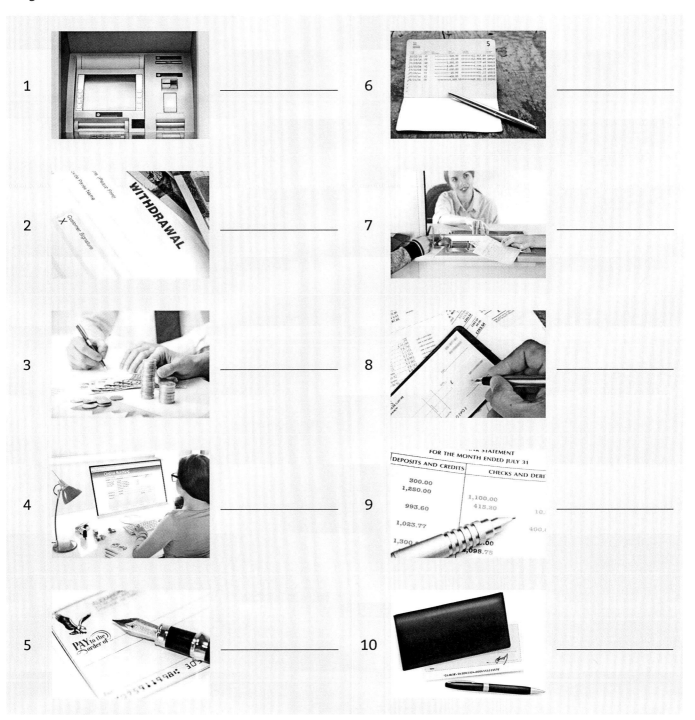

1 _____

2 _____

3 _____

4 _____

5 _____

6 _____

7 _____

8 _____

9 _____

10 _____

Matching Sentences and Illustrations

Read the sentences on page 80 and write the number of the sentence on the line that matches the illustration.

Pay attention to the **boldfaced** word.

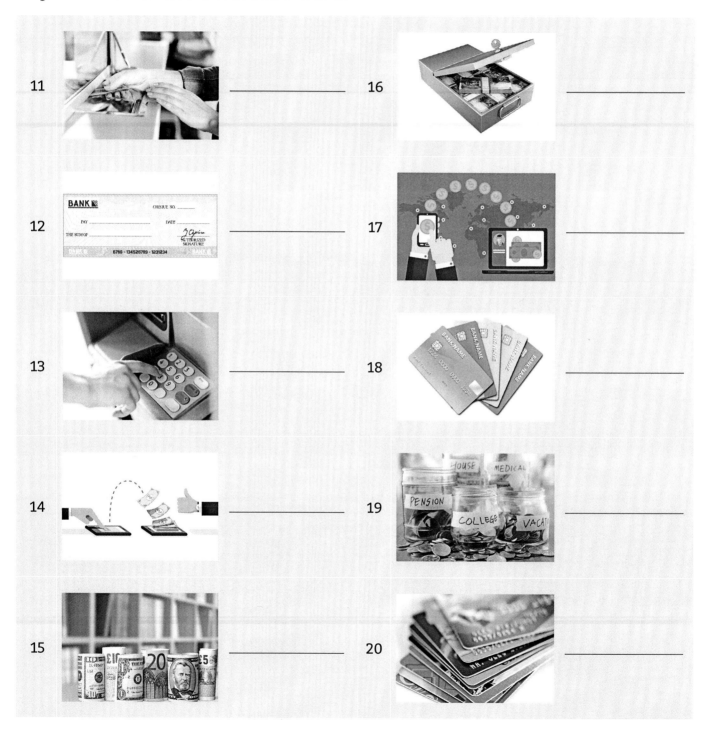

11 _____

16 _____

12 _____

17 _____

13 _____

18 _____

14 _____

19 _____

15 _____

20 _____

Lesson 9: At School

Read the vocabulary words and meanings aloud. Look at the illustrations and follow the strategies listed on page 12. Try using each word in a sentence out loud.

	Vocabulary Words/Meanings	Illustration
1	**Principal's office** The office of a school principal.	
2	**Classroom** A room where teachers instruct and students learn.	
3	**Gymnasium** A large room of a school used mostly for physical activities.	
4	**Library** A place where students read and borrow books.	
5	**Auditorium** A large room where speakers make speeches or entertainers perform.	

Read the vocabulary words and meanings aloud. Look at the illustrations and follow the strategies listed on page 12. Try using each word in a sentence out loud.

	Vocabulary Words/Meanings	Illustration
6	**Cafeteria** A place where students buy or eat lunch.	
7	**Secretary** The first employee people meet when they enter a school office.	
8	**Teacher** A person who instructs students.	
9	**Custodian** A worker who cleans the school.	
10	**Language Arts** A school subject in which students learn about words, their usage and literature.	

OTM18112 ISBN: 9781770788718 © On The Mark Press

Read the vocabulary words and meanings aloud. Look at the illustrations and follow the strategies listed on page 12. Try using each word in a sentence out loud.

Vocabulary Words/Meanings	Illustration
11 Science A school subject in which students learn about topics related to the physical world.	
12 Social Studies A school subject in which students learn about the relationship among people and nations.	
13 Mathematics A school subject studying numbers, their relationships, quantities, and measurements.	
14 Physical Education A school subject in which students participate in and study physical activities.	
15 Music A school subject in which students learn about the arrangement and production of musical sounds.	

Read the vocabulary words and meanings aloud. Look at the illustrations and follow the strategies listed on page 12. Try using each word in a sentence out loud.

	Vocabulary Words/Meanings	Illustration
16	**Biology** A school subject in which students learn about living things.	
17	**Chemistry** A high school subject in which students learn about the composition and properties of different substances.	
18	**Physics** A high school subject in which students learn about matter and energy.	
19	**French** A school subject in which students learn about Canada's official second language.	
20	**Computer Science** A school subject in which students learn about machines that store and process data.	

OTM18112   ISBN: 9781770788718 © On The Mark Press

Matching Vocabulary Words

language arts   chemistry   secretary   biology

science   teacher   gymnasium   library

principal's office   french

Match the illustrations with the vocabulary word. Write the name from the list above beside the picture.

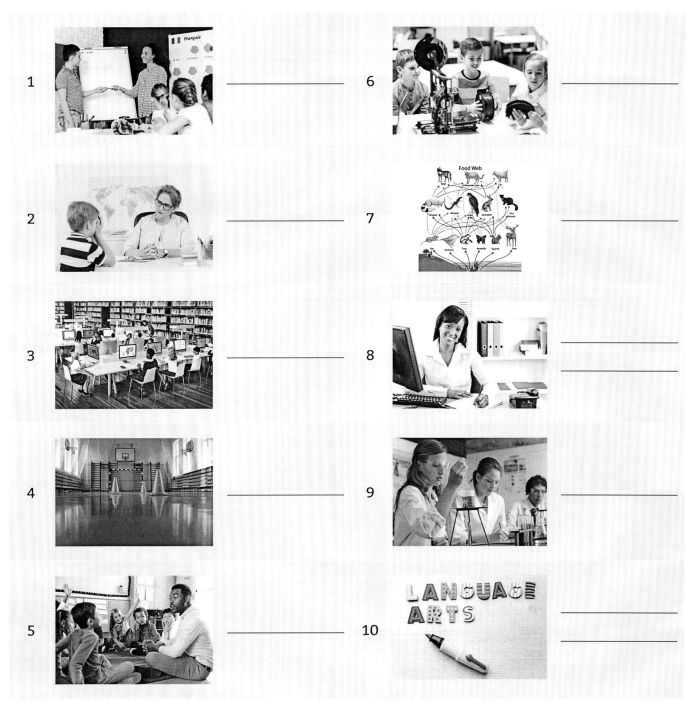

1 _____

2 _____

3 _____

4 _____

5 _____

6 _____

7 _____

8 _____

9 _____

10 _____

OTM18112 ISBN: 9781770788718 © On The Mark Press

Matching Vocabulary Words

physical education   mathematics   custodian   physics

cafeteria   music   auditorium   social studies

classroom   computer science

Match the illustrations with the vocabulary word. Write the name from the list above beside the picture.

11   _____

12   _____

13   _____

14   _____

15   _____

16   _____

17   _____

18   _____

19   _____

20   _____

OTM18112   ISBN: 9781770788718 © On The Mark Press

Matching Sentences and Illustrations

On the next page write the sentence on the line that matches the illustration. Pay attention to the **boldfaced** word.

a) My teacher sent me to the **principal's office**.

b) Each **classroom** has received new desks and chairs.

c) The games will begin shortly in the **gymnasium**.

d) All overdue books must be returned to the **library** by today.

e) Are the speeches being held in the **auditorium**?

f) At lunch time, there was a long lineup in the **cafeteria**.

g) Our school **secretary** called me to the office when my mom arrived.

h) Is your new **teacher** in his classroom?

i) Our new **custodian** helped me find my locker.

j) Those students have a **language arts** test today on parts of speech.

k) I left my log book in the **science** lab.

l) Did you use the globe to find Canada for the **social studies** project?

m) My **mathematics** mark improved after I wrote the geometry test.

n) The children are happy that **physical education** is offered daily.

o) I heard that the **music** students are going to a band camp.

p) Since taking **French**, my children have learned to speak Canada's second official language.

q) Tomorrow, my brother will be dissecting a frog in **biology** class.

r) Don't forget to memorize all the formulas in **chemistry**.

s) There will be questions about energy on the **physics** test.

t) Our class is going to the **computer science** classroom to use the new computers

Matching Sentences and Illustrations

Read the sentence on page 89 and write the number of the sentence on the line that matches the illustration.

Pay attention to the **boldfaced** word.

1 _____

2 _____

3 _____

4 _____

5 _____

6 _____

7 _____

8 _____

9 _____

10 _____

OTM18112   ISBN: 9781770788718 © On The Mark Press

Matching Sentences and Illustrations

Read the sentence on page 89 and write the number of the sentence on the line that matches the illustration.

Pay attention to the **boldfaced** word.

11 _____

12 _____

13 _____

14 _____

15 _____

16 _____

17 _____

18 _____

19 _____

20 _____

OTM18112   ISBN: 9781770788718 © On The Mark Press

Lesson 10: Medical Issues

Read the vocabulary words and meanings aloud. Look at the illustrations and follow the strategies listed on page 12. Try using the word in a sentence out loud.

	Vocabulary Words/Meanings	Illustration
1	**Headache** Pain in the head or face.	
2	**Sore throat** A painful, tender throat, often making it difficult to swallow.	
3	**Fever** A higher than normal body temperature.	
4	**Sprain** An injury caused when a person twists an ankle, elbow, knee or shoulder.	
5	**Diarrhea** Watery bowel movements that frequently cause pain.	

 OTM18112 ISBN: 9781770788718 © On The Mark Press

Read the vocabulary words and meanings aloud. Look at the illustrations and follow the strategies listed on page 12. Try using the word in a sentence out loud.

	Vocabulary Words/Meanings	Illustration
6	**Heart disease** A medical condition in which the heart does not work properly.	
7	**Hypertension** A medical condition in which blood pressure is higher than normal.	
8	**Rash** Red or pink spots on the skin.	
9	**Bleeding** Losing blood.	
10	**Cough** To force air out of the lungs.	

Read the vocabulary words and meanings aloud. Look at the illustrations and follow the strategies listed on page 12. Try using the word in a sentence out loud.

	Vocabulary Words/Meanings	Illustration
11	**Cold** An illness that consists of coughing and sneezing usually caused by a virus.	
12	**Diabetes** A medical condition in which blood sugar levels are higher or lower than normal.	
13	**Chest pain** Pain in the chest.	
14	**Vomit** Material that a person brings up from the stomach through the mouth.	
15	**Unconscious** Not awake or aware of the surroundings.	

OTM18112 ISBN: 9781770788718 © On The Mark Press

Read the vocabulary words and meanings aloud. Look at the illustrations and follow the strategies listed on page 12. Try using the word in a sentence out loud.

	Vocabulary Words/Meanings	Illustration
16	**Infection** A medical condition caused when germs and bacteria pass from one person to another.	
17	**Chills** A feeling of coldness.	
18	**Dizzy** An uncomfortable feeling everything is spinning.	
19	**Short of breath** Not taking adequate breaths.	
20	**Earache** A pain in the ear.	

Matching Vocabulary Words

| earache | cold | fever | sprain | dizzy |
| infection | cough | sore throat | diabetes | heart disease |

Match the illustrations with the vocabulary word. Write the name from the list above beside the picture.

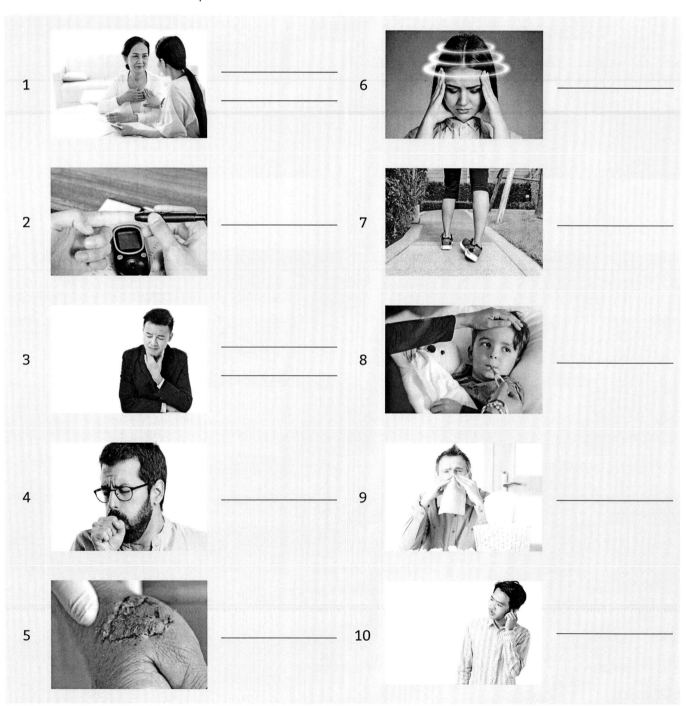

1 _____

2 _____

3 _____

4 _____

5 _____

6 _____

7 _____

8 _____

9 _____

10 _____

OTM18112 ISBN: 9781770788718 © On The Mark Press

Matching Vocabulary Words

unconscious   rash   short of breath   diarrhea   chest pain
hypertension   chills   vomit   headache   bleeding

Match the illustrations with the vocabulary word. Write the name from the
list above beside the picture.

11 _____

12 _____

13 _____

14 _____

15 _____

16 _____

17 _____

18 _____

19 _____

20 _____

OTM18112   ISBN: 9781770788718 © On The Mark Press

Matching Sentences and Illustrations

On the next page write the sentences on the line that matches the illustration. Pay attention to the **boldfaced** word.

a) Sometimes it is not easy to get rid of **a headache**.

b) He woke up this morning with a **sore throat**.

c) The baby was sweating all day with a **fever**.

d) My doctor says my injury is an ankle **sprain**.

e) The pharmacist suggested some medicine to stop the **diarrhea**.

f) Both of my sisters suffer from **heart disease**.

g) The doctor says my grandma has **hypertension** or high blood pressure.

h) The **rash** on the man's arm was related to his allergies.

i) How did you get the cut on your finger to stop **bleeding**?

j) Have you noticed that your **cough** is getting worse?

k) My **cold** was probably caused by a virus.

l) Several people in our family take medicine for **diabetes**.

m) They asked me at the hospital if I was having **chest pain**.

n) There are many causes of **vomiting**.

o) My neighbour was **unconscious** after falling on the floor.

p) Use a band-aid to prevent **infection** in that wound.

q) Do you have **chills** and a fever?

r) I was so **dizzy** that it looked like everything was spinning out of control.

s) After running upstairs, I was **short of breath**.

t) The child had an **earache** for two days.

OTM18112   ISBN: 9781770788718 © On The Mark Press

Matching Sentences and Illustrations

Read the sentence on page 98 and write the number of the sentence on the line that matches the illustration.

Pay attention to the **boldfaced** word.

1 _____

2 _____

3 _____

4 _____

5 _____

6 _____

7 _____

8 _____

9 _____

10 _____

Matching Sentences and Illustrations

Read the sentence on page 98 and write the number of the sentence on the line that matches the illustration.

Pay attention to the **boldfaced** word.

    OTM18112   ISBN: 9781770788718 © On The Mark Press

Lesson 11: Medications & Medical Procedures

Read the vocabulary words and meanings aloud. Look at the illustrations and follow the strategies listed on page 12. Try using the word in a sentence out loud.

	Vocabulary Words/Meanings	Illustration
1	**Prescription** Orders given by a doctor for a drug store to provide medicine for a person.	
2	**Doctor** A professional who studies medicine and becomes qualified to take care of patients' medical needs.	
3	**Tylenol or Ibprofin** Medication that relieves pain.	 Oleg Golovnev/Shutterstock.com
4	**Surgery** A procedure performed by a medical doctor called a surgeon.	
5	**Cough syrup** Medicine used to relieve coughing.	

Read the vocabulary words and meanings aloud. Look at the illustrations and follow the strategies listed on page 12. Try using the word in a sentence out loud.

	Vocabulary Words/Meanings	Illustration
6	**Patient** An individual who is receiving medical care or treatment.	
7	**Chest x-ray** A picture taken of the chest to look for medical conditions or illnesses.	
8	**Nurse** A medical professional who assists doctors and cares for the sick.	
9	**Needle** An instrument inserted into the body for medical purposes.	
10	**Chiropractor** A medical doctor skilled in treating conditions of the spine and joints.	

OTM18112 ISBN: 9781770788718 © On The Mark Press

Read the vocabulary words and meanings aloud. Look at the illustrations and follow the strategies listed on page 12. Try using the word in a sentence out loud.

Vocabulary Words/Meanings	Illustration
11 **Stitches** Movements made while inserting a needle into a wound or cut.	
12 **Heating pad** A piece of cloth heated by electricity used to relieve pain in the body.	
13 **Capsule** A tiny case containing medicine.	
14 **Blood test** A medical test used to analyze the chemistry and composition of a person's blood to determine illness or disease.	
15 **Injection** A procedure in which a needle is used to force fluid into the body.	

Read the vocabulary words and meanings aloud. Look at the illustrations and follow the strategies listed on page 12. Try using the word in a sentence out loud.

	Vocabulary Words/Meanings	Illustration
16	**Temperature** A measurement of hotness or coldness measured in degrees.	
17	**Ointment** A cream or lotion applied to the skin to relieve pain.	
18	**Specialist** A medical professional who specializes in a particular field of medicine.	
19	**Cough drops** Small material that looks like candy used to relieve a cough.	
20	**Physical therapy** Medical treatment provided by a physical therapist to relieve pain.	

OTM18112   ISBN: 9781770788718 © On The Mark Press

Name:

Matching Vocabulary Words

chiropractor   nurse   physical therapy   specialist   prescription

stitches   needle   chest-x ray   cough syrup   injection

Match the illustrations with the vocabulary word. Write the name from the list above beside the picture.

1 _____

2 _____

3 _____

4 _____

5 _____

6 _____

7 _____

8 _____

9 _____

10 _____

Matching Vocabulary Words

| doctor | cough drop | temperature | capsule | patient |
| ointment | tylenol | blood test | heating pad | surgery |

Match the illustrations with the vocabulary word. Write the name from the list above beside the picture.

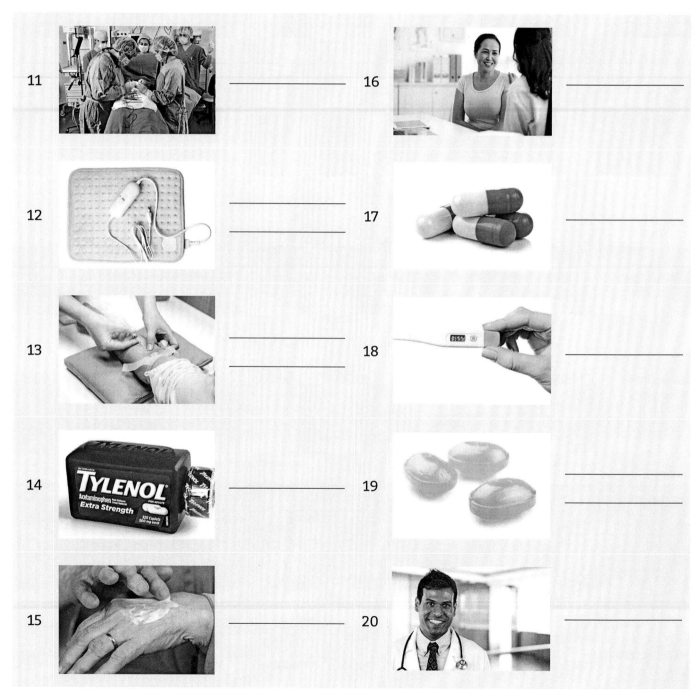

11 _____

12 _____

13 _____

14 _____

15 _____

16 _____

17 _____

18 _____

19 _____

20 _____

OTM18112   ISBN: 9781770788718 © On The Mark Press

Matching Sentences and Illustrations

On the next page write the sentence on the line that matches the illustration. Pay attention to the **boldfaced** word.

a) Do you need a new **prescription** from the drug store?

b) The **doctor** is still in the operating room.

c) Do you take **Tylenol or Ibuprofin** for headaches and other pain?

d) My grandpa had hip **surgery** today.

e) Take some **cough syrup** for your cold.

f) Our neighbour is a **patient** in that hospital.

g) Yesterday, the technician took me into that room for a **chest x-ray**.

h) My brother is a **nurse** at that clinic.

i) Go to the clinic and they will give you a **needle** containing a flu shot.

j) The **chiropractor** helped relieve the pain in my back.

k) Did the doctor give you **stitches** for the cut on your forehead?

l) Using a **heating pad** will soothe the pain in your neck.

m) My daughter cannot swallow medicine in **capsule** form.

n) Do you have to go to that clinic for a **blood test**?

o) My tummy was sore for two days after the **injection**.

p) Did your **temperature** increase when you were sick?

q) Ask the drug store for **ointment** to rub on that cut.

r) My family doctor is not a **specialist**.

s) Use these **cough drops** to help stop the coughing.

t) When I twisted my knee, the doctor recommended **physical therapy**.

Matching Sentences and Illustrations

Read the sentences on page 107 and write the number of the sentence on the line that matches the illustration. Pay attention to the **boldfaced** word.

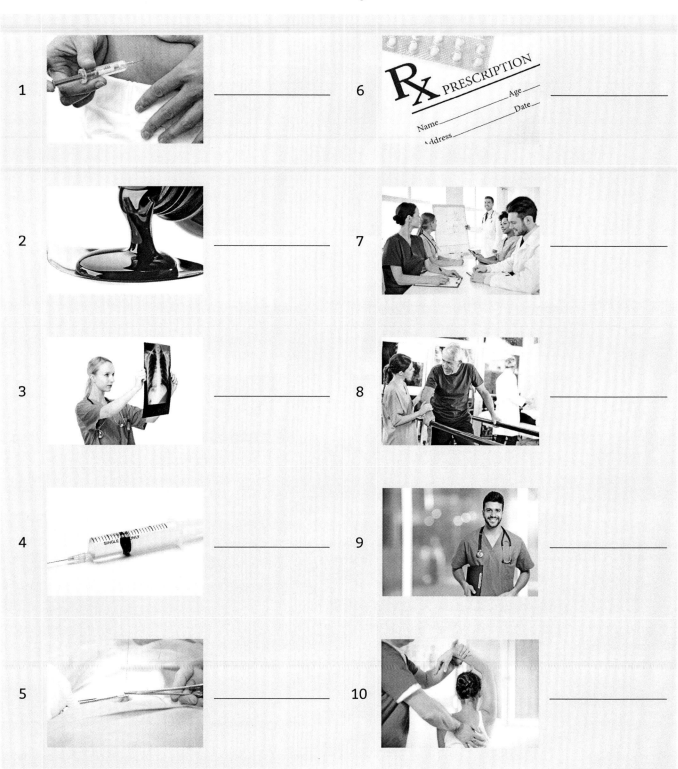

1 _____

2 _____

3 _____

4 _____

5 _____

6 _____

7 _____

8 _____

9 _____

10 _____

OTM18112   ISBN: 9781770788718 © On The Mark Press

Matching Sentences and Illustrations

Read the sentences on page 107 and write the number of the sentence on the line that matches the illustration. Pay attention to the **boldfaced** word.

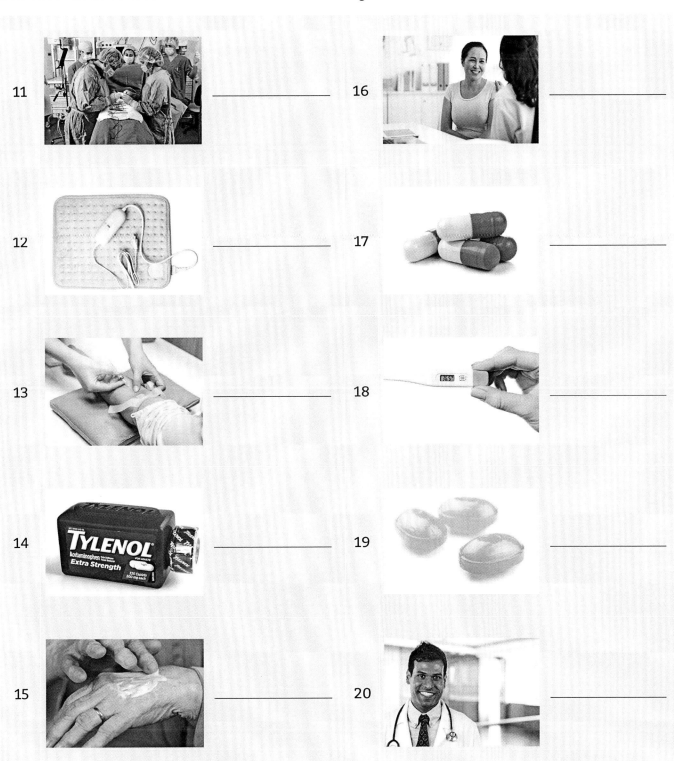

11 _____

16 _____

12 _____

17 _____

13 _____

18 _____

14 _____

19 _____

15 _____

20 _____

Lesson 12: Getting a Job

Read the vocabulary words and meanings aloud. Look at the illustrations and follow the strategies listed on page 12. Try using the word in a sentence out loud.

	Vocabulary Words/Meanings	Illustration
1	**Advertisement** A notice or display aimed at attracting customers.	
2	**Job skills** Skills that people use on jobs.	
3	**Educational history** A record of a person's education.	
4	**Shift work** Working at hours other than 8 to 4.	
5	**Available** Ready for use.	

OTM18112   ISBN: 9781770788718 © On The Mark Press

Read the vocabulary words and meanings aloud. Look at the illustrations and follow the strategies listed on page 12. Try using the word in a sentence out loud.

	Vocabulary Words/Meanings	Illustration
6	**Interview** To ask people questions to find out if they qualify for a job.	
7	**Professional attire** Dressed in a professional way.	
8	**Occupation** The business or profession a person studies and performs.	
9	**Hired** Employed.	
10	**Salary** Money a person receives for working.	

Read the vocabulary words and meanings aloud. Look at the illustrations and follow the strategies listed on page 12. Try using the word in a sentence out loud.

	Vocabulary Words/Meanings	Illustration
11	**Job Benefits** Money paid to an employee during times of illness, death or retirement.	
12	**Social Insurance Number** A number issued by the Canadian government that permits a person to work in Canada.	
13	**Resume** A summary of a person's employment history.	
14	**Full-time** Employed for approximately 40 hours per week.	
15	**Part-time** Employment for a certain number of hours, less than full time work.	

OTM18112   ISBN: 9781770788718 © On The Mark Press

Read the vocabulary words and meanings aloud. Look at the illustrations and follow the strategies listed on page 12. Try using the word in a sentence out loud.

	Vocabulary Words/Meanings	Illustration
16	**Casual** Working occasionally, when required.	
17	**Job application form** A document a person completes to apply for a job.	
18	**References** Statements others make about a person's suitability for a job.	
19	**Contact information** A person's phone, fax, or E-mail information.	
20	**Employment history** An individual's history of jobs, employment.	

Matching Vocabulary Words

| available | full-time | salary | hired | references |
| advertisement | shift work | part-time | resume | interview |

Match the illustrations with the vocabulary word. Write the name from the list beside the picture.

1 _____

2 _____

3 _____

4 _____

5 _____

6 Reference
  1 _____
  2 _____
  3 _____
  4 _____   _____

7 _____

8 _____

9 **40 HOUR WEEK MON. - FRI.**   _____

10 _____

OTM18112   ISBN: 9781770788718 © On The Mark Press

Matching Vocabulary Words

employment history   professional attire   social insurance number

occupation   contact information   job application form

job benefits   job skills   casual

educational history

Match the illustrations with the vocabulary word. Write the name from the list beside the picture.

11 _____

12 _____

13 _____

14 _____

15 _____

16 _____

17 _____

18 _____

19 _____

20 _____

Matching Sentences and Illustrations

On the next page write the sentence on the line that matches the illustration. Pay attention to the **boldfaced** word.

a) After I saw the **advertisemen**t, I decided to buy the items.

b) During the interview, I described my **job skills** and work history.

c) I listed my university courses in the **educational history** section of the application form.

d) Are you disappointed that you will be on **shift work** indefinitely?

e) When are you **available** to start this job?

f) I have a job **interview** this morning.

g) It is important to wear **professional attire** for job interviews.

h) What did you list as your **occupation**?

i) Only one of the applicants interviewed will be **hired**.

j) During the interview, you will find out the **salary** for this job.

k) **Job benefits** are very important to people seeking employment.

l) There is a place on the form for writing your **Social Insurance Number**.

m) Send your **resume** to several companies when looking for employment.

n) **Full-time** employment is 40 hours a week.

o) The **part-time** employees do not receive many job benefits.

p) My dad is not looking for **casual** employment.

q) The **job application form** is on your desk.

r) The company checked my job **references** before hiring me for the job.

s) Include all **contact information** on your job application form.

t) The applicant placed her **employment history** in chronological order.

OTM18112   ISBN: 9781770788718 © On The Mark Press

Matching Sentences and Illustrations

Read the sentences on page 116 and write the number of the sentence on the line that matches the illustration.

Pay attention to the **boldfaced** word.

1 _____

2 _____

3 _____

4 _____

5 _____

6 _____

7 _____

8 _____

9 _____

10 _____

Matching Sentences and Illustrations

Read the sentences on page 116 and write the number of the sentence on the line that matches the illustration.

Pay attention to the **boldfaced** word.

11 _____

12 _____

13 _____

14 _____

15 _____

16 _____

17 _____

18 _____

19 _____

20 _____

OTM18112   ISBN: 9781770788718 © On The Mark Press

Look at the pictures in the boxes. On the line, write the word that goes with the picture.

1. _____ _____

2. _____ _____

3. _____ _____

4. _____ _____

5. _____ _____

6. _____ _____

7. _____ _____

8. _____ _____

9. _____ _____

10. _____ _____

11. _____ _____

12. _____ _____

13. _____ _____

14. _____ _____

15. _____ _____

16. _____ _____

17. _____ _____

18. _____ _____

19. _____ _____

20. _____ _____

Word Search

cash	cheque	savings account	teller	safe deposit box
online banking	etransfer	deposit	currency	withdrawl
bankbook	PIN	transfer	money order	bank statement

Use the words from the list to complete the Word Search. The first one is done for you.

						h	s	a	c

OTM18112   ISBN: 9781770788718 © On The Mark Press

Unscrambling!

Unscramble the words and write the answers on the lines.

a.) milaecoiv_____

b.) voircnep_____

c.) taslop odec _____

d.) meoh ohnep mubern_____

e.) darssed_____

f.) ndeepnstde_____

g.) trnuocy _____

h.) hdtrtaibe _____

i.) lecl ohnep mubren _____

j.) narumse _____

k.) ylimaf _____

l.) gnilbiss _____

m.) uadthgrednarg_____

n.) toehrmdnarg_____

o.) taehrf_____

p.) htomre _____

q.) fdtaerhnagr_____

r.) tsreis _____

s.) torbehr _____

t.) dlihcern _____

Classification of Words

Siblings	Transfer	Cheque	Job skills	Deposit	Parents	Cash	Son
Headache	Family	Grandparents	Aunt	Available	Shift work	Hired	Salary
Money order	Fever	Credit card	Infection	Unconscious	Mother	Teller	Casual
Hypertension	Rash	Bleeding	SIN	Currency	Chest pain	Dizzy	Interview
Daughter	Occupation	Father	Brother	References	Online banking	Resume	bankbook

Write the vocabulary words in the correct column.

Family Words Banking Word

Family Words	Banking Words	Medical Words	Job Words

OTM18112   ISBN: 9781770788718 © On The Mark Press

Multiple Choice Test - *Test Your Vocabulary Knowledge!*

1. Did you call my house and leave a message on my _____?
   a. cell phone
   b. voicemail
   c. home phone
   d. address

2. The letter got lost because the sender forgot to include the _____.
   a. home phone number
   b. social insurance number
   c. postal code
   d. birthdate

3. I couldn't send you a message online because I didn't have your _____.
   a. email address
   b. social insurance number
   c. surname
   d. postal code

4. I will meet you by the mailbox on Maple _____.
   a. postal code
   b. Street
   c. province
   d. country

5. You didn't _____ the word correctly on the quiz.
   a. second
   b. spell
   c. dependents
   d. first

6. Last month, our _____ went crab fishing in Newfoundland.
   a. members
   b. family
   c. siblings
   d. birthdate

38. Take your backpack and go to your seat inside the _____.
   a. gymnasium
   b. auditorium
   c. classroom
   d. library

39. The basketball players were late arriving at the _____ for the game.
   a. library
   b. principal's office
   c. gymnasium
   d. classroom

40. The _____ will reopen after the book sale.
   a. cafeteria
   b. auditorium
   c. library
   d. gymnasium

41. Our _____ keeps our school very clean.
   a. secretary
   b. custodian
   c. teacher
   d. principal

42. Did your _____ assign a quiz today?
   a. principal
   b. secretary
   c. teacher
   d. custodian

43. Tomorrow, in _____ class, we will be doing an experiment on closed circuits.
   a. social studies
   b. science
   c. music
   d. computer science

7. His _____ took him to Disneyland during spring break.

   a. parents

   b. members

   c. siblings

   d. children

8. My _____ is my father's father.

   a. son

   b. uncle

   c. brother

   d. grandfather

9. My _____ was on the parcel, so the post office delivered it.

   a. home phone number

   b. E-mail address

   c. address

   d. cell phone number

10. My mother told me that she and her _____Lisa used to argue when they were growing up together.

    a. family

    b. sister

    c. aunt

    d. daughter

11. Bring the _____ inside when the magician arrives so they can see the act.

    a. aunt

    b. children

    c. uncle grandfather

    d. members

12. Are all the _____ of your family coming for Thanksgiving?

    a. grandmother

    b. members

    c. grandfather

    d. son

13. The leaves turned orange and yellow early this _____.

    a. spring

    b. fall

    c. winter

    d. summer

44. I heard an interesting presentation on the history of jazz in our _____ class.

    a. mathematics

    b. physical education

    c. music

    d. chemistry

45. Is your _____ class having a test on photosynthesis today?

    a. physics

    b. biology

    c. chemistry

    d. music

46. I forgot to study all the formulas, so my mark on the _____ test is low.

    a. biology

    b. health

    c. chemistry

    d. social studies

47. We visited the Ontario Legislature as part of our _____ program.

    a. mathematics

    b. social studies

    c. physics

    d. health

48. Even when I sat down, I was so _____ that the room kept spinning.

    a. cold

    b. dizzy

    c. unconscious

    d. bleeding

49. You were sweating so hard you must have had a _____.

    a. sprain

    b. cough

    c. rash

    d. fever

50. We have Tylenol in the medicine drawer if you think it will help your _____.

    a. headache

    b. rash

    c. cough

    d. infection

OTM18112   ISBN: 9781770788718 © On The Mark Press

14. It must be going to rain today as the sky looks very _____.
    a. white
    b. grey
    c. blue
    d. pink

15. My favourite season is _____ because I love to plant flowers.
    a. winter
    b. fall
    c. spring
    d. autumn

16. Wear your _____ pants as they match your black shoes.
    a. charcoal
    b. white
    c. black
    d. blue

17. The artist combined blue and green and created _____.
    a. fuchsia
    b. turquoise
    c. gold
    d. silver

18. Can you please pick me up after school? I will be standing by the door at _____.
    a. nine o'clock
    b. three o'clock
    c. seven am
    d. midnight

19. It snowed so hard _____ the roads were blocked for hours.
    a. next week
    b. tomorrow
    c. yesterday
    d. tomorrow night

20. There is going to be a full moon _____.
    a. tonight
    b. last week
    c. yesterday
    d. last night

51. The physical therapist says I have a knee _____.
    a. chills
    b. fever
    c. sprain
    d. earache

52. High blood pressure is another name for _____.
    a. sore throat
    b. diabetes
    c. hypertension
    d. heart disease

53. The child could not stop scratching because of the _____.
    a. cold
    b. rash
    c. sore throat
    d. earache

54. I was _____ when I stopped running at the top of the hill.
    a. cold
    b. dizzy
    c. unconscious
    d. short of breath

55. When the ambulance arrived, the passenger in the car was _____.
    a. fever
    b. unconscious
    c. sore throat
    d. infection

56. The child's leg was _____ from the dog bite.
    a. cough
    b. rash
    c. chills
    d. bleeding

57. I could hardly swallow when I had a _____.
    a. chest pain
    b. an earache
    c. a sore throat
    d. a sprain

21. The doctor arrived early for work at the _____.
    a. airport
    b. convenience store
    c. medical clinic
    d. dry cleaners

22. When did the _____ say you could file a claim for the accident?
    a. hospital
    b. dry cleaners
    c. restaurant
    d. insurance office

23. My brother works at a _____ called Macs.
    a. drug store
    b. grocery store
    c. convenience store
    d. shopping mall

24. The doctor told me to go to the _____ to get a prescription.
    a. drug store
    b. library
    c. office supplies store
    d. bank

25. Those dirty shirts need to go to the _____.
    a. gas station
    b. electronics
    c. hairdresser
    d. dry cleaners

26. When I walked into the _____, the clerk offered me a phone package.
    a. bookstore
    b. electronics store
    c. library
    d. grocery store

27. The clerk directed me to the _____ because I only had apples and grapes.
    a. customer service
    b. express checkout
    c. checkout
    d. supermarket

58. The drug store called to say the _____ is ready.
    a. prescription
    b. blood test
    c. surgery
    d. chest x-ray

59. It was the first time I received _____ in my forehead for a cut.
    a. stitches
    b. infection
    c. temperature
    d. patient

60. If you take some _____, it will relieve your cough.
    a. needle
    b. cough syrup
    c. heating pad
    d. physical therapy

61. My _____ helped relieve the pain in my wrist.
    a. chest-xray
    b. chiropractor
    c. cough drops
    d. needle

62. The nurse came to the school and gave the students a _____.
    a. needle
    b. ointment
    c. specialist
    d. cough syrup

63. My doctor sends me for a _____ every time I go for my physical exam.
    a. temperature
    b. capsule
    c. injection
    d. blood test

64. I give my daughter _____ when she has a headache.
    a. stitches
    b. ointment
    c. cough syrup
    d. Tylenol or Ibuprofin

OTM18112   ISBN: 9781770788718 © On The Mark Press

28. The clerk offered me a _____ until next week.
    a. checkout
    b. raincheck
    c. label
    d. self-checkout

29. The _____ fell off of the blanket, so I didn't know the price.
    a. shopping basket
    b. aisle
    c. label
    d. conveyor belt

30. When I placed my bananas on the _____, it started moving.
    a. conveyor belt
    b. coupon
    c. discount
    d. receipt

31. I kept the _____, so the store refunded my money.
    a. checkout
    b. aisle
    c. cash register
    d. receipt

32. When I presented this _____, the price dropped by ten percent.
    a. coupon
    b. aisle
    c. shopping basket
    d. shopping cart

33. We looked in the second _____, but we couldn't find the cereal.
    a. customer service
    b. self-checkout
    c. cash register
    d. aisle

34. Are you paying for this purchase with _____ or cheque?
    a. withdrawl
    b. deposit
    c. cash
    d. currency

65. Another name for getting a needle is an _____.
    a. heating-pad
    b. specialist
    c. injection
    d. patient

66. Our _____ stopped working, so I had to suffer with knee pain.
    a. heating pad
    b. blood test
    c. temperature
    d. resume

67. Before going for _____ on my elbow, it pained every day.
    a. patient
    b. specialist
    c. physical therapy
    d. temperature

68. The _____ stated that the job was part-time.
    a. advertisement
    b. resume
    c. job benefits
    d. employment history

69. If your _____ is not impressive, you will not get an interview.
    a. resume
    b. professional attire
    c. shift work
    d. salary

70. Most of the applicants were not _____ to work on weekends.
    a. casual
    b. available
    c. references
    d. educational history

71. I will transfer some money from my savings account into my _____ tomorrow.
    a. chequing account
    b. PIN
    c. chequebook
    d. deposit

35. When I receive cheques, I _____ them into my account immediately.

    a. withdrawl

    b. money order

    c. cheque

    d. deposit

36. The clerk handed me a printout of my _____.

    a. safe deposit box

    b. deposit

    c. withdrawl

    d. bankbook

37. My parents opened their _____ today to take outs some important documents.

    a. ATM Machine

    b. PIN

    c. safe deposit box

    d. online banking

72. The money in this country is a different colour and an unfamiliar _____.

    a. e-transfer

    b. money order

    c. currency

    d. transfer

73. When you get your _____, apply for the job.

    a. shift work

    b. salary

    c. Social Insurance Number

    d. PIN

74. This business hires full-time and _____ employees.

    a. references

    b. contact information

    c. interview

    d. part-time

OTM18112   ISBN: 9781770788718 © On The Mark Press

ANSWER KEY

Vocabulary Matching			
Lesson 1 - Pages 16-17	**Lesson 2 – Pages 26-27**	**Lesson 3 – Page 34**	**Lesson 4 – Pages 42-43**
1-Postal code	1-Siblings or Brother	1-Seven; seventh	1-Gold
2-First name	2-Nephew	2-Ten; tenth	2-Black
3-Middle initial	3-Granddaughter	3-Eight; Eighth	3-Green
4-Surname	4-Family	4-Nine; ninth	4-Fuchsia
5-Dependents	5-Brother or Siblings	5-Six; sixth	5-Spring
6-Spell	6-Grandfather	6-Two; second	6-Fall
7-Address	7-Father	7-Four; fourth	7-Winter
8-Country	8-Grandson	8-One; first	8-Autumn
9-Town/city	9-Members	9-Five; fifth	9-Grey
10-Business phone number	10-Grandmother	10-Three; third	10-Blue
11-Social insurance number	11-Aunt		11-Red
12-Street	12-Children		12-Beige
13-Province	13-Daughter		13-White
14-Sex/gender	14-Sister		14-Charcoal
15-Birthdate	15-Uncle		15-Pink
16-Voicemail	16-Parents		16-Silver
17-Cell phone number	17-Grandparents		17-Orange
18-Home phone number	18-Mother		18-Purple
19-Email address	19-Son		19-Summer
20-Avenue	20-Niece		20-Turquoise
Lesson 5 – Pages 51-52	**Lesson 6 – Pages 60-61**	**Lesson 7 – Pages 69-70**	**Lesson 8 – Pages 78-79**
1-Six twenty	1-Airport	1-Coupon	1-ATM
2-Evening	2-Restaurant	2-Shopping cart	2-Withdrawal
3-Two fifteen	3-Shopping mall	3-Express checkout	3-Cash
4-One o'clock	4-Gas station	4-Aisle	4-Online banking
5-Tonight	5-Drug store	5-Self-checkout	5-Money order
6-This week	6-Library	6-Cash register	6-bankbook
7-Noon	7-School	7-Meat manager	7-Teller

8-Eight pm	8-Hospital	8-Label	8-Chequing account
9-Ten after nine	9-Hairdresser	9-Customer	9-Bank statement
10-Three thirty	10-Grocery store	10-Clerk	10-Chequebook
11-Last night	11-Convenience store	11-Raincheck	11-Deposit
12-Today	12-Office Supplies store	12-Discount	12-Cheque
13-Midnight	13-Bus stop	13-Supermarket manager	13-Personal identification number (PIN)
14-Next week	14-Dry cleaners	14-Checkout	14-E-transfer
15-Morning	15-Medical clinic	15-Receipt	15-Currency
16-Five after five	16-Insurance office	16-Cashier	16-Safe deposit box
17-Yesterday	17-Train station	17-Customer service	17-Transfer
18-Seven am	18-Place of worship	18-Conveyor belt	18-Debit card
19-Tomorrow	19-Bank	19-Produce manager	19-Savings account
20-Four forty-five	20-Electronics store	20-Shopping basket	20-Credit card
Lesson 9 – Pages 87-88	**Lesson 10 – Pages 96-97**	**Lesson 11 – Pages 105-106**	**Lesson 12 - Pages 114-115**
1-French	1-Heart disease	1-Injection	1-Interview
2-Principal's office	2-Diabetes	2-Cough syrup	2-Resume
3-Library	3-Sore throat	3-Chest x-ray	3-Part-time
4-Gymnasium	4-Cough	4-Needle	4-Shift work
5-Teacher	5-Infection	5-Stitches	5-Advertisement
6-Science	6-Dizzy	6-Prescription	6-References
7-Biology	7-Sprain	7-Specialist	7-Hired
8-Secretary	8-Fever	8-Physical therapy	8-Salary
9-Chemistry	9-Cold	9-Nurse	9-Full-time
10-Language arts	10-Earache	10-Chiropractor	10-Available
11-Computer science	11-Bleeding	11-Surgery	11-Educational history
12-Classroom	12-Headache	12-Heating pad	12-Job skills
13-Globe	13-Vomiting	13-Blood test	13-Job benefits
14-Auditorium	14-Chills	14-Tylenol or Ibuprofen	14-Casual
15-Music	15-Hypertension	15-Ointment	15-Job application form
16-Cafeteria	16-Chest pain	16-Patient	16-Contact information

OTM18112   ISBN: 9781770788718 © On The Mark Press

17-Physics	17-Diarrhea	17-Capsule	17-Occupation
18-Custodian	18-Short of breath	18-Temperature	18-Social Insurance Number
19-Mathematics	19—Rash	19-Cough drops	19-Professional attire
20-Physical education	20-Unconscious	20-Doctor	20-Employment history

Sentence Matching
Answers indicate the vocabulary word that is used in the sentence to match the picture.
Example Sentence: My **address** in Halifax is 416 Haliburton Road. The answer is **address**.

Lesson 1 – Pages 19-20	Lesson 2 – Pages 29-30	Lesson 3 – Pages 36-37	Lesson 4 – Pages 45-46
1-Postal code	1-Brother	1-Ten	1-Gold
2-First name	2-Nephew	2-tenth	2-Two
3-Address	3-Granddaughter	3-One	3-Green
4-Dependents	4-Family	4-Fifth	4-Summer
5-Spell	5-Siblings	5-Six	5-Spring
6-Business phone number	6-Grandfather	6-Seven	6-Fall
7-Middle initial	7-Father	7-Three	7-Winter
8-Surname	8-Grandson	8-Seventh	8-Autumn
9-Country	9-Members	9-Ninth	9-Grey
10-Town/city	10-Grandmother	10-Two	10-Blue
11-Social Insurance Number	11-Aunt	11-Third	11-Red
12-Street	12-Children	12-Four	12-Beige
13-Home phone number	13-Daughter	13-Eight	13-White
14-Email address	14-Sister	14-Five	14-Charcoal
15-Avenue	15-Uncle	5-Sixth	15-Pink
16-Birthdate	16-Parents	16-Nine	16-Silver
17-Voicemail	17-Grandparents	17-First	17-Orange
18-Cell phone	18-Mother	18-Fourth	18-Purple
19-Sex/gender	19-Niece	19-Eighth	19-Fuchsia
20-Province	20-Son	20-Second	20-Turquoise

Lesson 5 – Pages 54-55	Lesson 6 – Pages 63-64	Lesson 7 – Pages 72-73	Lesson 8 – Pages 81-82
1-Six twenty-five	1-Airport	1-Coupon	1-ATM machine
2-Evening	2-Restaurant	2-Shopping cart	2-Withdrawl
3-Two fifteen	3-Shopping mall	3-Customer	3-Cash
4-One o'clock	4-Gas station	4-Aisle	4-Online banking
5-Last night	5-Drug Store	5-Self checkout	5-Money order
6-Next week	6-Library	6-Cash register	6-Bankbook
7-Today	7-School	7-Meat Manager	7-Teller
8-Eight pm	8-Hospital	8-Label	8-Chequing account
9-Ten after nine	9-Hairdresser	9-Express checkout	9-Bank statement
10-Three thirty	10-Grocery store	10-Clerk	10-Chequebook
11-Midnight	11-Convenience store	11-Raincheck	11-Deposit
12-Tonight	12-Office supplies store	12-Discount	12-Cheque
13-Noon	13-Bus stop	13-Supermarket Manager	13-Personal Identification Number (PIN)
14-Yesterday	14-Dry cleaners	14-Checkout	14-E transfer
15-This morning	15-Medical clinic	15-Receipt	15-Currency
16-Five after five	16-Insurance office	16-Cashier	16-Safe deposit box
17-Tomorrow	17-Train station	17-Customer service	17-Transfer
18-Eight pm	18-Place of worship	18-Conveyor belt	18-Debit card
19-This week	19-Bank	19-Produce manager	19-Savings account
20-Four forty five	20-Electronics store	20-Shopping basket	20-Credit card

Lesson 9 – Pages 90-91	Lesson 10 – Pages 99-100	Lesson 11 – Pages 108-109	Lesson 12 – Pages 117-118
1-French	1-Heart disease	1-Injection	1-Job interview
2-Principal's office	2-Diabetes	2-Cough syrup	2-Resume
3-Library	3-Sore throat	3-Chest x-ray	3-Part-time
4-Gymnasium	4-Cough	4-Needle	4-Shift work
5-Teacher	5-Infection	5-Stitches	5-Advertisement
6-Science	6-Dizzy	6-Prescription	6-References
7-Biology	7-Sprain	7-Specialist	7-Hired
8-Secretary	8-Fever	8-Physical therapy	8-Salary
9-Chemistry	9-Cold	9-Nurse	9-Full-time work
10-Language arts	10-Earache	10-Chiropractor	10-Available

OTM18112   ISBN: 9781770788718 © On The Mark Press

11-Computer science	11-Bleeding	11-Surgery	11-Educational history
12-Classroom	12-Headache	12-Heating pad	12-Job skill
13-Globe	13-Vomiting	13-Blood test	13-Job benefits
14-Advertisement	14-Chills	14-Tylenol or Ibuprofen	14-Casual
15-Music	15-Hypertension	15-Ointment	15-Job application
16-Cafeteria	16-Chest pain	16-Patient	16-Contact information
17-Physics	17-Diarrhea	17-Capsule	17-Occupation
18-Custodian	18-Short of breath	18-Temperature	18-Social Insurance Number
19-Mathematics	19-Rash	19-Cough drops	19-Professional Attire
20-Physical education	20-Unconscious	20-Doctor	20-Employment history

Review # 1 – Page 119

Full Time Work	Interview	Job application form	Resume	Social insurance number
Prescription	Doctor	Patient	Nurse	Chiropractor
Temperature	Capsule	Heating pad	Gymnasium	Library
Cafeteria	Secretary	Teacher	Custodian	Debit card

Review # 3 – Page 121

Voicemail	Province	Postal code	Home phone number	Address
Dependents	Country	Birthdate	Cell phone number	Surname
Family	Siblings	Granddaughter	Grandmother	father
Mother	Grandfather	Sister	Brother	Children

Multiple Choice Test – Pages 123-128

1. b	2. c	3. a	4. b	5. b	6. b	7. a	8. d
9. c	10. b	11. b	12. b	13. b	14. b	15. c	16. a
17. b	18. b	19. c	20. a	21. c	22. d	23. c	24. a
25. d	26. b	27. b	28. b	29. c	30. a	31. d	32. a
41. b	42. c	43. b	44. c	45. b	46. c	47. b	48. b
49. d	50. a	51. c	52. c	53. b	54. d	55. b	56. d
57. c	58. a	59. a	60. b	61. b	62. a	63. d	64. d
65. c	66. a	67. c	68. a	69. a	70. b	71. a	72. c
73. c	74. d						